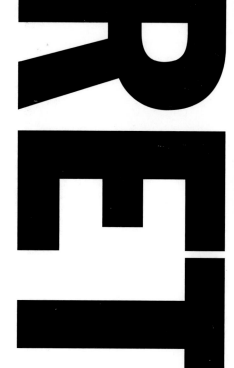

CRETE

SPIRALGUIDE

AA Publishing

Contents

Written by Donna Dailey and Mike Gerrard
Revised and updated by Lara Dunston

Revision managed by Bookwork Creative Associates
Series Editor Karen Rigden
Series Designer Catherine Murray

Published by AA Publishing, a trading name of AA Media Limited,
whose registered office is Fanum House, Basing View, Basingstoke,
Hampshire RG21 4EA. Registered number 06112600.

ISBN: 978-0-7495-5968-7

The content of this book is believed to be accurate at the time of
printing. Due to its nature the content is likely to vary or change and
the publisher is not responsible for such change and accordingly
is not responsible for the consequences of any reliance by the
reader on information that has changed. Any rights that are given
to consumers under applicable law are not affected. Opinions
expressed are for guidance only and are those of the assessor based
on their experience at the time of review and may differ from the
reader's opinions based on their subsequent experience.

We have tried to ensure accuracy in this guide, but things do
change, so please let us know if you have any comments at
travelguides@theAA.com.

A CIP catalogue record for this book is available from the British
Library.

Cover design and binding style by permission of AA Publishing
Colour separation by Keenes, Andover
Printed and bound in China by Leo Paper Products

Find out more about AA Publishing and the wide range of services the
AA provides by visiting our website at theAA.com/shop

A04682
Maps in this title produced from mapping © Freytag-Berndt u.
Artaria KG, 1231 Vienna-Austria
(except pp157 & 159)

The Magazine

A great holiday is more than just lying on a beach or shopping till you drop — to really get the most from your trip you need to know what makes the place tick. The Magazine provides an entertaining overview to some of the social, cultural and natural elements that make up the unique character of this engaging island.

FIRST A CRETAN,
then a Greek

Crete's beloved author Nikos Kazantzakis declared he was "first a Cretan, then a Greek", and this is a belief still shared by Cretans of all ages, from all walks of life, and from all corners of the island.

Cretans spent decades striving for *enosis* (union) with Greece, achieved in 1913, yet it was motivated not by a desire to reconnect with their roots, but by a need to protect their land. Security concerns stemmed from the Battle of Crete and a long history of invasions. Physically separated from the rest of the country by the Sea of Crete, Greece's largest island has always been vulnerable.

Crete's centuries of resistance to foreign occupation (➤ 16–19) and its tireless struggle for freedom have left a deep imprint on the soul. Cretans are survivors who fiercely value their independence and self-reliance. During local festivals and celebrations men wear costumes with a dagger or firearm tucked into their waist sash, symbolising their readiness to resist and the value of freedom and *philotimo* (honour) in Cretan tradition.

SYMBOL OF MOURNING
You'll notice old women wearing black. Traditionally, Cretans wore black for three years out of respect for a dead relative. Foreign oppression brought such loss and mourning that it virtually became the national colour.

ELEFTHÉRIOS VENIZÉLOS

Crete's revered statesman Elefthérios Venizélos (1864–1936) was one man who didn't hesitate to resist. Born in Mournies village near Chania, he fought against Turkish rule and in 1897 led a protest that saw the first raising of the Greek flag on Crete. Venizélos became prime minister of Greece in 1910 and under his rule *enosis* was achieved. Streets and squares throughout Greece bear his name.

ALL IN THE FAMILY

To understand the Cretan character, look to the bedrock of island life – the land and the family. Family means extended family and it's not uncommon for several generations to live together under one roof and for family members to help each other in times of need.

Socially, different generations mix happily in and outside of the home. Don't be surprised to see youths in the latest fashions and hip haircuts sitting beside moustachioed grandfathers in baggy breeches and high boots at a local bar. Though young people are increasingly leaving rural areas to study or work in cities, most return to the village for Easter, family celebrations, festivals and harvests.

WHAT'S IN A NAME?

Some 2,000 years ago, Cretan philosopher Epimenides said all

Mosque interior, Venetian Fortress, Rethymno

Cretans were liars, St Paul quoted him, and it stuck. Most likely the claim stems from an ancient Cretan belief in a fertility god who died and was reborn annually. The Cretan "Zeus" was buried beneath Mount Giouchtas near Knossos, but the northern Greeks, for whom their Zeus was immortal, were outraged by this heresy and branded them liars.

What is true is that Cretans enjoy a good story. They love to talk and can be prone to exaggeration and making promises that might be forgotten the next day. It's all part of their mercurial nature – alternately warm and indifferent, relaxed and passionate, but always genuine.

A STRANGER AND A GUEST

The Greek word *xenoi* has a dual meaning: "stranger" and "guest". It is the custom that a stranger is automatically a guest in one's country and in one's home. Although the high tourist numbers threaten this tradition, expect to experience sudden gestures of hospitality – fresh figs from someone's tree, a complimentary *rakí*, an invitation to share a meal. Such generosity doesn't need to be repaid, for Cretans take pleasure in giving. Show your appreciation with a smile and a simple *efharisto* (thanks in Greek).

CRETAN INSTITUTIONS

The *kafeníon* (café), a coffeehouse-cum-bar, is to Crete what the pub is to Britain. There's at least one in every village or town and you'll recognise it by the men sitting outside drinking strong Greek coffee or brandy, playing cards or backgammon, exchanging news, and arguing politics.

The *kafeníon* is a male domain, as much an unofficial men's club as a
public café, and although few Cretan women buck tradition by joining the
men, exceptions are made for visitors. These days, local women, along
with the younger generation, prefer to drink their Nescafé *frappés* in the
many stylish contemporary cafés that line the waterfronts and squares of
Cretan cities and towns.

You'll also notice that chairs generally face outwards to the street rather
face each other. Cypriots enjoy people-watching and love nothing more
than to watch the *voltá*, or evening stroll. Introduced by the Venetians, the
voltá is a time for socialising and a chance to dress up and see and be
seen. Whether around the town square or along a seafront promenade,
families and couples stroll arm in arm, stopping to chat with friends, while
groups of young people gossip and flirt.

Spend some time in one place and you'll quickly appreciate Crete's
strong café culture and the rituals and cycles of business at different cafés
throughout the day – one crowded with old ladies in the morning might
be closed by the afternoon, while another that looks shut down will be
buzzing with students by night.

Café culture in Chania (left) and contrasting rural life on the Omalos Plain (above)

THE RITUAL-LOVING
MINOANS

The ancient Minoans, were an aesthetic, creative, ritual-loving people, if we can believe the pretty scenes depicted on pottery, frescoes and mosaics at Crete's museums and archaeological sites.

Crete was home to the Minoans, Europe's first civilisation, from around 3000 BC when their culture flourished, until 1100 BC. Amazingly, evidence of its greatness lay hidden until the 20th century when Englishman Arthur Evans excavated Knossos (► 76–80). Evans named the Minoans after the mythical Greek King Minos. It turned out that "Minos" was not a name but a title, like Egypt's pharaoh or Rome's caesar, and some 22 rulers bore this name.

These priest-kings built extravagant palaces at Knossos, Phaistos, Malia and Zakros, where they presided over a rich artistic culture that was obsessed with rituals.

THE ART OF LIFE

Most of what we know about the Minoans has been gleaned from their beautiful artworks. Vivid frescoes once decorated the walls of palaces, depicting scenes from Minoan life. These vibrant, paintings, made colourful from plants, minerals and shellfish, were skilfully executed, incorporating dynamic movement and sensuality. Women's skin was painted white and men's red, suggesting women may have played a powerful role in society or spent their days as ladies of leisure while the men worked outside toiling the fields.

Exquisite sculptures, pottery, mosaics and decorative arts suggest that the Minoans lived an ancient version of the "good life". Their palace homes had roof terraces, light wells, baths and sophisticated plumbing systems. They were well fed, with huge granaries and giant vessels called *pithoi* which stored wine and olive oil. They were also great seafarers, trading their agricultural produce far and wide to acquire copper and tin to produce bronze, and gold, silver and precious stones to create jewellery and works of art.

THE MINOAN AGES

Archaeologists break down the Minoan civilisation into four main periods:

■ Pre-Palace period (2600–1900 BC). Bronze Age culture develops on Crete.
■ Old Palace period (1900–1700 BC). First Minoan palaces built but destroyed by earthquakes.
■ New Palace period (1700–1450 BC). Grand new palaces built and the civilisation reaches its height.
■ Post-Palace period (1450–1100 BC). Minoan civilisation declines and Mycenaeans move in.

Visitors stroll along the Royal Way

One of the most curious facts about the Minoan's palaces is that they were built without fortifications, suggesting they lived peacefully and didn't fear attacks from enemies.

DANCES WITH BULLS

Greece may be the birthplace of the Olympic games, but long before the first torch was carried through a stadium the Minoans were apparently turning somersaults over the horns of charging bulls. The Minoans loved games and athletic contests and bull-leaping satisfied both their appetite for sport and religious obligation. Images on artworks suggest that Minoan athletes would grab a charging bull by the horns, somersault over its back, and land on their feet with arms raised in victory, and that both men and women took part in these dramatic feats, requiring great courage, agility and skill.

Spanish bullfighters claim bull-leaping is impossible, leading some scholars to suggest the scenes may only be symbolic. Representing virility, bulls had great significance in Minoan society. They were shaped into figurines and painted on vases, enormous sculpted "horns of consecration" adorned palace walls, and ceremonial drinking vessels called *rhytons* were carved into the shape of a bull's head.

THE SNAKE GODDESS

A potent Minoan religious figure that you'll see in figurines in museums and shops was that of the Snake Goddess, a woman holding a snake in each hand. Her bare breasts symbolised fertility while the snake, which sheds its skin, symbolised healing and rebirth.

In sacrificial rites related to agricultural cycles, a bull was captured and bound, its throat cut and its blood drained into the sacred cups. The ritual was thought to honour the bull and connect Minoans to their divine life force. Whether or not it actually occurred, bull-leaping may have symbolised the triumph of man over the forces of nature.

A DISASTROUS ENDING

Excavated giant storage vessel

However, the Minoans weren't to triumph and their civilisation came to a sudden end around 1450 BC, when a catastrophe occurred that destroyed all of their palaces. Many believe the volcanic eruption on nearby Santorini (Thira) created a deluge of tidal waves, earthquakes and fires on Crete, which could explain the charred remains found at palaces. Other scholars favour theories of invaders, such as the Mycenaeans, or a rebellion against the palace rulers. Whatever the cause, within 200 years the Minoans had all but disappeared; the reason remains a mystery.

MYTH OF THE MINOTAUR

Legend has it that Poseidon, god of the sea, sent King Minos a white bull, but when he later requested it be sacrificed Minos couldn't bring himself to kill the beautiful animal. In revenge the angry god caused the king's wife, Pasiphae, to fall in love with the bull and their mating produced the Minotaur, a creature with a bull's head and man's body. Minos kept the monster in a labyrinth beneath the palace and every nine years 14 youths were shipped from Athens and fed to the Minotaur. When Theseus, son of Athens' king, heard of this he vowed to stop the slaughter. Volunteering to be one of the victims, he entered the palace, seduced Minos's daughter Ariadne, who gave him a sword and ball of thread with which to kill the bull, and miraculously found his way out of the labyrinth.

THE
BEAT
OF
CRETE

Watch a performance of live music in a restaurant or bar and witness how the locals are moved to tears and passionately join in for the chorus, and you'll appreciate how deeply music is embedded in the Cretan soul.

THE *MANTINADA*, *RIZITIKA* AND *EROTOKRITI*

Dating back to the 5th century BC, the *Mantinada* is made up of rhyming couplets containing 15 syllables. The songs typically express every kind of emotion, especially the extremes of joy and sadness related to love.

Another popular musical form is *Rizitika* or rebel music. Originating in the White Mountains in the Chania province, the songs are mostly performed at weddings, baptisms and celebrations.

Erotokriti are folk songs derived from the 10,000-line *Erotokritos* (tried by love) epic written by Vitsentzos Kornáros (➤ 111) in the 16th century. Singers in Crete often perform songs based on parts of the *Erotokritos*, although some have been known to perform the whole poem in concert!

THE INSTRUMENTS OF MUSIC

The key instruments of Cretan music that you'll see used are the *lyra* and *laouto*. The *lyra* is a three-stringed, pear-shaped instrument, traditionally made of mulberry wood and played on the knee like an upright violin. It's normally accompanied by the *laouto*, a type of lute that has four pairs of strings. These days the *laouto* is popular as a solo instrument as well.

The *lyra* player will often sing as well and will alternate between singing passages and soloing on the instrument, while the *laouto* accompanies. The traditional music is a unique mix, sometimes sounding like an Irish jig and at other times like sounds reminiscent of the Middle East.

WHERE TO SEE LIVE MUSIC

Live music performed on these revered instruments is still immensely popular, especially in Rethymno and Chania. Look for tavernas that have images of musical instruments on their signs outside and you're pretty much assured that at some stage of the night – whether it's planned or spontaneous (often there are instruments hanging on the walls!) there will be a performance.

On a good night, a performance can last for hours with much improvising and trading of complex musical motifs between the musicians. The intoxicating mix of the music coupled with the effects of a few shots of *rakí* makes for a memorable night out! Weekends are the best times to hear live music and one of the more atmospheric places to see musicians is at O Gounas taverna in Rethymno.

MUSICAL MASTERS

The music shops of Iraklio (➤ 69) are a good source of authentic Cretan music. Look out for Nikos Xilouris (one of the greatest players), and his brother Antonis, known as Psarantonis. Thanassis Skordalos is another contender for the title of "the greatest".

FOREIGN INFLUENCES
& Exotic Flavours

Crete's unique social character and exotic flavour is the result of centuries of foreign influence, from the demise of the Minoans until the early 20th century. Successive occupations have shaped the architectural landscape, complex cuisine, heartfelt music, and strength of character of the Cretan people.

When you're sitting in a café in Crete, people-watching, watch the Cretans at the next table for a while. You'd be forgiven for mistaking them for Italians with their stylish dress, confident demeanour, and hand gesturing, and their musical Cretan dialect even sounds more Italian than Greek. Watch a traditional three-piece band perform in a taverna and you'll detect Turkish and Arab influences in the music. And in the cuisine – the Cretan *mezedes* are very similar to those served up in Turkey and the Middle East.

THE GREEKS

Mycenaean warriors from the Peloponnese were the first to invade Crete, rebuilding Minoan palaces such as Knossos and other settlements. As their power waned, the northern Greek Dorians moved in to establish city-states, which you can see at Gortys, Lato and elsewhere. The original Cretans retreated to the mountains, which is why these days villagers from the interior make claims to be the purest Cretans.

THE ROMANS

Conquering Crete in 67 BC, the Romans established their capital at Gortys (▶ 81–83) and built aqueducts, irrigation systems, roads, odeons, theatres, and pretty arched stone bridges, one of which you can see at Vrisses, 32km (20 miles) from Chania. St Paul brought Christianity to Crete in AD 59.

Left: Rocco al Mare fortress, Iraklio
Right: Minaret of Nerantzes Mosque, Rethymno

TIMELINE

1450–1100 BC Mycenaean period
1100–67 BC Dorian period
67 BC–AD 337 Roman rule
337–824 First Byzantine period
824–961 Arab occupation
961–1204 Second Byzantine period
1204–1669 Venetian period
1669–1898 Ottoman period
1898 Crete gains autonomy
1913 *Enosis* (union) with Greece
1941–5 German occupation during World War II

THE BYZANTINES

With the fall of the Western Roman Empire, Crete became part of the Byzantine Empire, ruled from Constantinople. During the first and second Byzantine periods, Christianity and art flourished and splendid monasteries and churches were built, many still standing today, such as the exquisite Arkadi and Preveli monasteries, and the churches in the Rethymno region.

THE ARABS

The Saracens, a band of Arabs who had been expelled from Spain and Alexandria, captured Crete in the 9th century. Gortys and other cities were destroyed, and Chandax (Iraklio) became a pirate den and slave market. The Byzantine general Nikefóras Fokás retook the island in 961 after a grisly siege in which captured Saracens were decapitated and their heads catapulted over the fortress walls. Little remains of this dark period.

Weathered pantiles on the roofs of the italianate church at Epano Episkopi, near Sitia

Dionysius and Ariadne moasic in Chania's Archaeological Museum

THE VENETIANS

Following the breakup of the Byzantine Empire, Crete was sold to Venice for 1,000 pieces of silver. Venetian rule, which lasted 465 years, brought prosperity, culture and the great fortresses, harbours, mansions, buildings, and fountains which you can see in Rethymno, Chania and Iraklio.

THE OTTOMANS

The Ottomans first attacked Chania in 1645, but it was another 24 years before they occupied Crete. Under Ottoman rule the island fell into economic and artistic decline and Christians were persecuted. The Cretans continuously rebelled, launching attacks from mountain strongholds. Splendid stone mosques with pretty minarets, and wooden Ottoman buildings boasting hanging balconies remain from this period, in Rethymno and Chania.

WHAT'S IN A NAME?

Crete's capital Iraklio has been known by many names. A port under the Romans, called Herakleium, after the Arab conquest it was fortified and named Rabdh-el-Khandak (Castle of the Moat) or Chandax. In medieval times the Venetians called the city and island Candia, while under Ottoman rule, it was Megalo Kastro (Great fortress). Iraklio (Iraklion, Heraklion) was adopted in 1922.

Writers and Artists

The Greeks invented literature with the *Odyssey* and the *Iliad* and created some of the world's most exquisite Byzantine painting, but the Cretans can be thanked for producing three of the world's most celebrated artists, the influential painter El Greco, the much-admired author Nikos Kazantzakis, and the Nobel Prize-winning poet Odysseus Elytis.

ODYSSEUS ELYTIS, THE POET

The Cretan poet Odysseus Elytis (1911–96) was born in Iraklio to a wealthy family from the island of Lesbos, home to the ancient poetess Sappho, a source of inspiration to Elytis. His poetry was musical in form and rich in imagery inspired by myths and legends. While his earlier poems celebrated nature and the senses, his later, darker, work focused on suffering and grieving. Becoming a popular war poet, Elytis wrote potently about his experiences fighting the Germans during World War II. He was awarded the Nobel Prize for Literature in 1979.

EL GRECO, THE PAINTER

Born in the village of Fodele on Crete in 1541 (▶ 88) the painter Domenikos Theotokopoulos would spend most of his life overseas, becoming known wherever he lived as The Greek, or El Greco. An artist of immense talent, he studied under one of the greatest Cretan painters of the day, Michael Damaskinos, whose best works can be seen in the Icon Museum in Iraklio (▶ 60–61). At the age of 27, Theotokopoulos moved to Venice to further his studies and pursue the art of icon painting. There he successfully combined the Byzantine style that he had mastered on Crete with the

> He achieved fame as a fine sculptor...as well as an artist

Renaissance style that was prevalent in Italy. After almost ten years in Italy with limited commercial success, he moved to Toledo, Spain, where he lived for the most part until his death in 1614. It was there he achieved

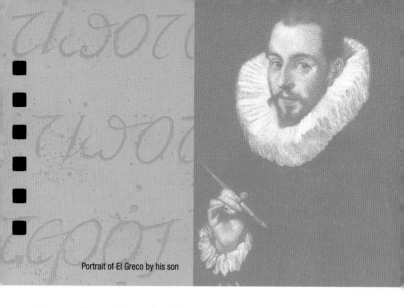

Portrait of El Greco by his son

fame as a fine sculptor and architect as well as an artist. Several of his paintings are in the National Gallery in Athens, but only one can be seen on his native island, in the Historical Museum in Iraklio (▶ 58–59).

NIKOS KAZANTZAKIS, THE WRITER

Crete's legendary writer Nikos Kazantzakis (1883–1957; pictured below) called his autobiography *Report to Greco*, in a nod to his great forebear. Born in Iraklio in 1883, Kazantzakis is forever associated with the character he created for his 1946 novel, *Zorba the Greek*. Widely regarded as signifying the robust Cretan character, Zorba was in fact a mainland Greek who came to Crete and showed the locals how to live.

The author's ambivalence to his fellow islanders – he spent most of life away from Crete – is shown in *Christ Recrucified*, in which Cretan villagers tear each other apart while the Turkish rulers stand by.

Despite his conflicting emotions about Crete Kazantzakis was proud of the island. At his request, he was buried in Iraklio and his grave stands on top of the Martinengo Bastion on the city walls. His epitaph reveals much about the Cretan character: "I hope for nothing. I fear nothing. I am free."

THE BATTLE
OF CRETE

The Battle of Crete began with the biggest airborne assault in military history. So determined was Hitler to capture the island that he launched an offensive on 20 May 1941 that turned the sky polka dot with planes and paratroopers.

In what was known as Unterrnehmen Merkur (Operation Mercury), tens of thousands of German soldiers invaded the island in an event that lives on in the mind of every Cretan through stories passed down from those alive at the time to new generations. Crete was a valuable strategic stronghold and the British prime minister, Winston Churchill, described it as his island fortress, believing it to be impregnable. And for some time the Allied naval forces succeeded in keeping German forces at bay.

OPERATION MERCURY

At the time of the invasion some 32,000 Allied troops (British, Australian and New Zealand) were recuperating on Crete, having been evacuated from Greece and the Balkan countries. The Italian army had invaded the Greek mainland in October 1940, and with German help had pushed their

way through the country, forcing the evacuation of troops to Crete. Crete's location in the southern Mediterranean, offering access to Greece, North Africa and the Middle East, meant it was tactically important. So in order to secure it, Hitler took to the skies in an audacious and dramatic move.

THE BATTLE BEGINS

At 6am on 20 May the initial bombardment began. At 8am, after a short lull, another wave of planes flew over. And at 8:15am thousands of paratroopers began filling the skies, concentrating at first on Chania and the important airfield nearby at Maleme. German losses were initially heavy as ordinary Cretans rushed to help the troops defend their island.

CASUALTIES

Official casualty figures necessarily include estimates and probably underestimate the numbers involved. Greek figures aren't known, but the German air corps recorded taking 5,255 Greek prisoners. The Allied forces reported 1,751 killed, with 1,738 wounded, and 12,254 prisoners of war. In addition, the Allied naval forces estimated that well over 2,000 seamen died. The Germans estimated about 4,000 men killed or not accounted for, and another 2,600 wounded. It seems likely that at least 10,000 people died during the battle, and many more during the 1941–45 German occupation of Crete.

The Allied War Cemetery at Souda

Men, women and children, armed with pitchforks, old rifles and makeshift weapons killed many of the invaders before they had time to untangle their parachutes after floating to earth.

While the first day had not gone well for the Germans, their decision to concentrate on taking the airport the next day bore fruit and the sheer scale of the attack proved too much for the Allied forces. After several hours of heroic defence the Germans seized Hill 107, a strategic position that enabled them to take control of the airfield. After this, German planes were able to land and bring in more troops and weaponry.

IT'S AN ENIGMA

German troops were also landing at Iraklio and Rethymno, although it took them until 31 May to capture Rethymno. By this time the Allies

PATRICK LEIGH FERMOR

British travel writer Patrick Leigh Fermor was an intelligence officer in the British Army, serving on Crete. After the German invasion he lived in the Cretan mountains for two years and, disguised as a shepherd, helped co-ordinate the Cretan resistance. In 1944 he was responsible for the audacious kidnap of the German Commander on Crete, General Kreipe (▶ 88–89, Anogia). *Ill Met by Moonlight*, written by Fermor's fellow conspirator, W Stanley Moss, tells how the resistance fighters succeeded in kidnapping Kreipe from the very heart of German headquarters, spiriting him away to the mountains and eventually taking him off the island to Egypt for interrogation.

A child's drawing of The Battle of Crete, displayed in the Naval Museum of Crete

were in retreat, crossing the White Mountains, heading down the Impros Gorge and evacuating to Egypt from the little port of Chora Sfakion. Cretan resistance, however, didn't stop with the withdrawal of the Allied troops. It continued courageously until the end of the war.

The battle was not only strategically important, it was significant because of Hitler's use of masses of paratroopers, the resistance shown by civilians, and the fact that the Allies were expecting the invasion, having cracked the German's Enigma code for encrypting messages. How the Allies were defeated by the Germans after being forewarned remains a controversial and often heated subject of discussion.

Several significant sights related to the battle are the Maritime Museum of Crete at Chania (➤ 136–137), the monastery Moni Preveli (➤ 144) and the Allied War Cemetery at Souda (➤ 148).

LOSING THE BATTLE, WINNING THE WAR

Although Hitler had planned to start his invasion of Russia in April 1941, he decided instead to prioritise the task of capturing Crete and thus delay the attack on Russia until June. While taking Crete was important to Hitler, it may have been a decision that cost him the war, because as a result of the delay his armies had not captured Moscow or Leningrad (St Petersburg) by the time the harsh Russian winter struck.

When Hitler ordered his southern troops to attack Stalingrad (now Volgograd), a quarter of a million German soldiers were killed or wounded, a defeat from which Hitler's army never fully recovered.

Though they lost the Battle of Crete, the Allies went on to defeat the Germans and win the war.

Eat Drink and Be Merry

Cretan cuisine is as tasty as it is healthy, blending pulses, olive oil, fruit and vegetables, and fresh fish and seafood – all washed down with the island's robust red wine. The keys to Cretan cooking are seasonality and simplicity.

FRUIT AND VEGETABLES

The diet's strength is its emphasis on fresh vegetables and Cretans consume three times as many vegetables as other Europeans, with artichokes, tomatoes, cucumbers, spinach, aubergines, beans, carrots, potatoes and leeks all organically grown on the island. They also eat several times more fruit than other Europeans and you'll find fresh fruit offered at every opportunity – especially oranges, which grow prolifically on the island.

FISH AND SEAFOOD

The island's long, thin shape means that you're never too far from the sea and a supply of fresh seafood – and Cretans love nothing more than a seafood feast. You'll find swordfish, tuna, bream, sea bass, mullet, squid, whitebait and sardines on offer, all caught locally.

OLIVE OIL

Crete produces wonderful olive oil and it's used almost to the complete exclusion of butter and other fat products. Crete's extra virgin olive oil tastes so delicious that it's almost a sin that it's so good for you.

WINE AND SPIRITS

You'll find wine on the table of almost every meal after breakfast in Crete, however, Cretans drink in moderation. The local wines, both white and red, perfectly match the cuisine. You'll also find two clear spirits offered in most restaurants and bars: *tsikoudia* (a brandy-like Crete speciality made from the pips, skins and stems of grapes used to make wine) and *ouzo* (an aniseed-flavoured aperitif).

WHAT TO EAT

Apart from regional specialities such as wild boar and rabbit, you'll find most taverna menus to be similar. Locals usually start with a salad such as the classic Greek salad (tomatoes, onion, cucumber, olives and feta cheese), followed by grilled fish or moussaka (aubergine and minced lamb casserole). The perennial favourite is *souvláki* (meat grilled on a skewer) of which chicken, lamb and pork are popular.

THE CRETAN DIET

Research begun in 1956 by American nutritionist Dr Ancel Keys compared diets, diseases and death rates in seven countries, including Japan, Italy and the US. Greek studies were undertaken in Corfu and Crete, with Crete showing by far the lowest mortality rates for heart diseases and cancer. In Finland, for example, there were 972 such deaths per 100,000 people in 1986, whereas the figure for Crete was just 38, the lowest in the world. Dr Keys was so impressed by this data that he followed the Cretan Diet himself – all the way to age 100.

THE CRETAN HABITAT
and its creatures

Crete's landscape – and its flora and fauna – has been changed considerably by human habitation. As you explore the island today, it's still possible to enjoy breathtaking scenery and sight some spectacular creatures.

THE HEART-STOPPING CRETAN HABITAT

Crete's defining natural features are its spectacular mountains, covering two-thirds of its surface. Four colossal limestone ranges dominate the centre from the east coast to the west. The highest and most dramatic are the Lefka Ori, or White Mountains, in the west; the central Psiloreitis range, with the highest peak; and in the east, the Dikti and Sitia ranges.

Carved into the mountains are some awe-inspiring gorges. Samaria is Crete's most famous gorge (➤ 140–141), but others also offer rewarding – and less crowded – hikes, such as the Imbrou Gorge (➤ 145), northeast of Chora Sfakion; Kotsifou Gorge, north of Plakias; Kourtaliotiko Gorge, north of Moni Preveli; and Aradena Gorge, west of Loutro.

PLUNDERED FORESTS

Looking at Crete's landscape today, often covered in stubby kermes oak and *phrygana* (a low scrub), it's hard to imagine the whole island was once densely forested with cedar and cypress. The seafaring Minoans were the first to fell trees – using the timber for ships and buildings – and the Venetians and Turks continued the deforestation. Today only pockets of native woodland exist.

Along the tree line (1,650m/5,414 feet) of the southern White Mountains are cypresses over 1,000 years old. Not only are they among the oldest trees in Europe but early signs of coppicing suggest they may also be the world's oldest managed forest.

COLOURFUL AND AROMATIC

Growing wild on many hillsides are aromatic herbs such as oregano, thyme, sage, and marjoram and you'll often see locals gathering these herbs. Cretan dittany, or _díktamo_, is a medicinal herb that grows in remote gorges, used in ancient times to heal arrow wounds and ease childbirth pains.

In spring the countryside is ablaze with colour as wildflowers bloom in every field and crevice. One third of Greece's 6,000 plant species are found on Crete, of which nine per cent are endemic. One of the more unusual is _Phoenix theophrasti_, a native date palm (➤ 117). Several

---

THE FACTS

Surface area: 8,300sq km/3,200sq miles.

Length east to west: 250km/155 miles.

Width north to south: 60km/37 miles (widest), 12km/7 miles (narrowest).

Highest peak: Mount Ida (Psiloreitis), 2,456m/8,058 feet.

Longest gorge: Samaria, 18km/11 miles.

Longest river: Geropotamos, on the Mesara Plain, 45km/30 miles.

dozen African and Asiatic species, as well as plants from the Balkans and Western Europe, can also be found here. Above all, Crete is renowned for its wild orchids – there are some 67 varieties growing on the island – and bulbs, including wild tulips, Cretan iris and Cretan ebony.

SOME OF ITS CREATURES

Sadly, with the loss of its natural forest habitat, Crete's deer and many other larger woodland species of mammal largely died out, but the small hardy, endemic Cretan spiny mouse (with its characteristic back spines) remains notable.

Another animal you may see is the *kri-kri*, sometimes called *agrimi*, a large wild goat with sweeping horns much like those of an ibex. Its summer coat is reddish-brown, and males have a rather large beard. Once plentiful, it was often depicted in Minoan art but was hunted to near extinction. The only natural population left is in remote areas of the White Mountains and the Samaria Gorge (► 140–141).

Crete's geographical position and diverse habitats of high coastal cliffs, rocky islets, wetlands and meadows make it a mecca for birdlife. Out of Greece's 420 species, 350 have been spotted on Crete, and the island is also a stopover for winter migrants.

A small village rises above the Lasithiou Plain

Crete is the last breeding ground in Greece for the rare and endangered lammergeier, or bearded vulture. This magnificent bird has a wingspan up to 3m (10 feet). Only a few breeding pairs remain but the vulture is occasionally spotted above the Omalos or Lasithiou plateaux. You are more likely to spot the more common griffon vulture, with its distinctive white head.

ENDANGERED SPECIES

The Cretan wildcat, *fourokattos* (furious cat), was assumed to be a myth until a team studying carnivorous animals accidentally trapped this elusive, nocturnal animal in 1996. Weighing 5.5kg (12lb), with a tawny coat and tiger-like growl, it's not in fact related to the cats of mainland Greece or Europe but to a North African species. The cat was radio-collared, studied and set free, but it's not known if there are any more.

The beaches west of Rethymno, west of Chania and around Matala are important breeding grounds for the loggerhead sea turtle. The Sea Turtle Protection Society of Greece (www.archelon.gr) operates a conservation programme, with kiosks at these resorts to raise public awareness. Most in danger of extinction, though, is the Mediterranean monk seal, which has been seen around islets off the coast.

Goats graze on a hillside pasture

ICONS
OF THEIR TIME

Icon painting is a great Cretan tradition and the island's artists became renowned for the genre from the 15th to 17th centuries under the name of the Cretan School.

Icons were being painted for many centuries before this, of course, but during that period Cretan artists were in great demand in Venice, the artistic capital of the western world. The Cretan School reached a peak around the Fall of Constantinople in 1453, with many artists relocating to Crete and the island became a centre for the art.

The icon painting of the Cretan School was renowned for the balance of the compositions, the strong use of colour in the garments of the subjects and the sharp lines of the brushstrokes. The School's fame spread widely throughout the 16th century and the painters organised themselves into guilds. A master of one was no less than El Greco (➤ 20–21) – at the ripe old age of 22.

An artist continues the tradition of icon painting on Crete

A fine example of Cretan icon art

Painters in the Cretan School were often versatile, being able to paint *alla greca*, in the Byzantine style, as well as *alla latina*, referring to the Renaissance style that El Greco later became famous for.

A SKILL FOR TODAY

Today icon painting is a skill that is still highly respected on Crete, though few artists today create icons in the traditional way. The frame for an icon painting must be made from a hard, dry wood like oak, chestnut or pine, not an oily wood such as the olive tree. The paper is handmade from cotton. Egg and vinegar are used to make the egg tempura, and 23-carat gold leaf provides the background. Paints are also handmade in the traditional way, with dyes derived from minerals, plants and metals.

The best place to see the classic icon paintings is at the Icon Museum in Iraklio (➤ 60–61). If you're inspired to buy or commission a new icon painting, make sure that the painter is using traditional methods.

FESTIVALS

Cretans love a festival. There are public and religious holidays, Saints' Days, and festivals devoted to arts, culture, wine, sultanas – and even chestnuts!

JANUARY
6 January: Feast of the Epiphany and Blessing of the Waters celebrated in ports.

MARCH
Carnival celebrated around Crete with street parties 40 days before Easter (see below), notably in Sitia and Rethymno.

APRIL
23 April: Feast of Agios Giorgios, St George, patron saint of shepherds, with village feasts.
Easter: The biggest Orthodox festival with processions building up to Saturday night Mass and feasting Easter Sunday; dates vary (different from Christian Easter).

MAY
20 May: The Battle of Crete, commemorated in Chania.

SUMMER
Summer festivals around Crete, notably Iraklio's Summer Arts Festival, Sitia's cultural festival Kornaria, and Rethymno's Wine Festival and Renaissance Festival.

AUGUST
25 August: Feast of Agios Titos, Crete's patron saint, celebrated across Crete.
Mid-August: Sitia Sultana Festival, involving much imbibing and feasting.

OCTOBER
Mid-October: Chestnut Festival in western Crete and Elos village (► 167).
28 October: Ochi Day, celebrated throughout Greece, commemorating Greek General Metaxas' one-word response *ochi* (no) to Mussolini's request to allow Italian troops into Greece in 1940.

DECEMBER
6 December: Feast of Agios Nikolaos, patron saint of seafarers, celebrated in Agios Nikolaos (► 106–107) and around Crete.

Finding Your Feet

First Two Hours

Arriving

The two main points of entry are both on the north coast of Crete. Iraklio, the capital, serves the centre and east of the island and Chania, the second city, serves the west. Both have ferry ports and international airports. Iraklio is served by more airlines and ferries so may be more convenient from that point of view, but if your main interest is in visiting the west of Crete, try to arrange to arrive at Chania.

A third airport capable of taking international flights is at Sitia. It would be worth checking flights here if you wish to visit the less busy eastern end of the island.

It takes about two hours to drive the 160km (100 miles) between Iraklio and Chania along the good New Road (National Highway), which runs for most of the length of Crete's north coast. While most visitors to Crete organise a rental car, which they tend to pick up and drop off at the airport, there is also a good bus service between the two cities and they are both major centres for the extensive bus network, making it fairly easy and inexpensive to get around the island.

Iraklio Airport

■ The airport is **5km (3 miles) east of the city centre** (tel: 2810-228402).
■ **Bus No 1** leaves from in front of the terminal for the city centre every few minutes from 6am to 11pm. The fare is about €1.50.
■ **Numerous taxis** can always be found outside the airport. Beware of touts and go to the official taxi rank.
■ Check that the fare is **metered** and the meter switched on, or agree the fare beforehand. Take time to find the board at the taxi rank that lists the approximate fares to most popular destinations (another reason not to go with a tout).
■ A **taxi into Iraklio** should cost about €15 (higher after midnight) with a small charge for baggage.
■ **Money exchange facilities**, **car-rental offices**, plenty of **luggage trolleys**, **shops**, **bars** and **cafés** are available at the airport.
■ If you are **renting a car**, the airport is close to the New Road. Follow signs for Agios Nikolaos if you are heading east, or for Iraklio and then Rethymno if heading west. Iraklio city centre is about a 15-minute drive away.
■ If you need to **park** at the airport for any length of time, use the large and inexpensive public car park directly opposite the terminal building on the far side of the road.
■ Unfortunately **delays** are common in summer on charter flights. There is far more room on land-side than air-side, so don't go through passport control until you need to.
■ Depending on the season, there are as many as **15 flights a day** to Athens, a journey which takes just under one hour.
■ There are **regular services** to Thessaloniki, Rhodes, Santorini (Tra), Paros, Mykonos, Larnaca and Rome.
■ Most **domestic flights** are operated by the national carrier, Olympic Airways (tel: 2810-229191), and Aegean Airlines (tel: 80 111 20000), so shop around. These airlines offer regular services.

Chania Airport

■ The airport is **near Souda**, about 15km (9 miles) northeast of the city centre (tel: 28210-63264).

- **Public buses** meet incoming flights but there is no regular service and most people take a taxi.
- **Taxis** are numerous and a ride into the city centre should cost about €15, more with baggage. See above for precautions to take when getting a taxi.
- **Money exchange** offices, car-rental desks, shops and cafés are all available at the airport.
- There are **several flights a day** connecting with Athens, from the national carrier Olympic Airways and Aegean Airlines.
- Aegean Airlines also operates **regular flights** to Thessaloniki.
- If you are **renting a car**, follow signs for Souda to reach the New Road and avoid central Chania; otherwise follow signs for Chania to reach the city centre. When you reach the New Road, turn left to head east marked Rethymno and Iraklio and turn right to head west. This is marked Chania but bypasses the city centre.

Sitia Airport
- The airport is about **2km (1 mile) northwest of the centre** (tel: 28430-24424; www.sitia-airport.com).
- **Taxis** meet incoming flights. The fare into Sitia should be about €10.

Iraklio Harbour
- The commercial harbour lies **slightly to the east** of the town centre.
- The walk between the two is not long, but if you have **heavy luggage** you would be advised to take a taxi.
- There are **daily ferries** to Athens and Santorini (Thira), and in season frequent sailings to the Cycladic Islands, the Sporades and Thessaloniki.
- For **information** contact the Port Authority (tel: 2810-244912).

Chania Harbour
- **Ferries** dock at the harbour near Souda, which is about a 20-minute drive east of the city centre. **Taxis** are available.
- There is a **daily ferry service** to Athens.
- For **information** contact the Port Authority (tel: 28210-98888).

Tourist Information Offices
Tourist offices can only be found in the large towns. Where there isn't one, try travel agencies for information. They keep sporadic hours and are often closed during the winter.
National Tourist Office (Iraklio): Odas Xanthoudidou 1, tel: 2810-22803, opposite the Archaeological Museum.
Chania: Kydonias 29–31, tel: 28210-92943.
Rethymno: Dimocratias 1, tel: 28310-225012.
Agios Nikolaos: I. Koundourou 21A, beside the bridge in between lake and harbour, tel: 28410-22357.
Sitia: on the waterfront, tel: 28430-28300.

Admission Charges
The cost of admission to museums and places of interest mentioned in the text is indicated by price categories.
Inexpensive under €3   **Moderate** €3–€5 **Expensive** over €4

Getting Around

Travelling around Crete is easy provided you are not too ambitious. It is a big island, and if you want to spend some time relaxing then the best advice is to limit yourself to one region.

Bus Services

■ Bus services are **generally good**. There are, for example, roughly 25 buses per day between Iraklio and Chania and a similar number between Iraklio and Agios Nikolaos.

■ The **best services** are between the major towns and major tourist resorts. Buses here are usually frequent and comfortable. In more remote places, you may find older buses in use, with a service restricted to an early morning bus into the main town, and an afternoon bus back again.

■ Services are **operated by KTEL**, and buses are pale blue. In larger towns there is often more than one bus station, so check which one you need.

■ Tickets should be bought in advance at the bus station. In smaller places where the "bus station" is merely a parking spot, the nearest shop will often sell tickets. Look for signs or ask.

■ A **timetable** for the whole of Crete is produced each year, which is available from bus stations and travel agents. However, double-check times if possible, as services do change.

■ You can check timetables in advance by visiting the KTEL website: **www.bus-service-crete-ktel.com**

Taxis

■ Taxis on Crete are **comparable to Greece** and continental Europe and people use them for quite long journeys.

■ Taxis are **metered** but it is common to agree a price for a particular journey. Always do this in advance.

■ **Taxi ranks** should carry display a board showing price guides to the most popular destinations.

Ferries

■ For travelling within Crete, ferries are **not usually the best option** as there are reasonably good roads and a good bus network.

■ There is one exception: travelling along the south coast. In summer **a regular service operates** from Palaiochora in the west to Agia Galini further east, stopping at Sougia, Agia Roumeli and Chora Sfakion on the way. This is much easier than taking buses inland and around the mountains if you do not have your own transport.

■ A ferry operates from Palaiochora to the **offshore island of Gavdos**.

■ The **major ports are on the north coast** at Iraklio, Chania, Sitia, Agios Nikolaos and Kastelli Kissamou. All except the last have ferry connections to Piraeus for Athens and to other Greek islands, while Kastelli Kissamou is the best for services to the Peloponnese.

Driving

■ Most of the **main roads** are of a decent standard, the best being the E75 highway, that links towns along Crete's north coast. This is invariably signposted as the New Road, but is also called the National Highway.

■ Off the main road **standards vary enormously**, and even on major roads you should watch out for unexpected pot-holes or rock-fall.

■ On many main roads the **right-hand "lane"** is actually a wide shoulder, used for pulling on to when a car wishes to overtake.

- It is always best to ask locally about **road conditions**, as roads which may appear to be good on maps can turn out to be rutted tracks, and conditions can change in bad weather.
- Many locals drive down **the middle of the road**. Keep well in to your side of the road. Reckless overtaking is common, even on blind bends.
- Another **driver flashing his headlights** at you means that he is coming through, NOT that he is giving way to you. Either that, or he is warning you there is a police speed trap around the corner.
- The **beeping of horns** is very common, but it can simply mean the driver has seen a friend walking by, or is tooting as he passes a relative's shop, so don't assume it is directed at you.

Driving Essentials

- Drive on the **right-hand** side of the road.
- Wearing **seatbelts** where fitted is compulsory, but many locals ignore this rule. Don't be tempted to copy them.
- **Children** under ten must not sit in the front seat.
- **Drink-driving** is a serious offence. A blood-alcohol level of only 0.05 per cent means a heavy instant fine, and over 0.08 per cent is a criminal offence and can lead to imprisonment. The police sometimes set up random breath-testing checkpoints. The best advice is not to drive if you want to have a drink.
- The **speed limit** is 120kph (74mph) on highways, 90kph (55mph) on other main roads and 50kph (31mph) in urban areas. These limits may vary slightly so watch for the speed-limit signs.
- **Vehicles coming from the right** have right of way, even on roundabouts.

Car Rental

- All main towns and tourist resorts, and airports, have several **car-rental companies** competing for business.
- **Rates** on Crete are higher than the European average, but local firms tend to under-cut the major international names.
- In theory, an **international driving licence** is required, but in practice a valid national driving licence will suffice for most companies; check when you make your reservation.
- **Minimum age** varies from 21 to 25, depending on the rental company's policy.
- Rental rates often include **third-party insurance** and **unlimited mileage**, but it is advisable to also take out coverage for CDW (Collision Damage Waiver).
- Rental companies **usually ask for a deposit** by credit card or in cash.
- If renting in **late summer or autumn**, it may be worth paying extra for a recognised name such as Hertz or Europcar, whose vehicles probably have a better service record.

Bringing Your Own Car

- You are allowed to take your own car to Crete for a period of **up to six months** or until the tax or insurance expires.
- EU citizens **no longer need a Green Card**.
- These rules change regularly on Crete so check with a **motoring organisation** such as the AA (www.theAA.com) for up-to-date information and advice.

Breakdowns

- Car-rental companies will **provide an emergency number** to contact.
- Dial 104 for emergency help anywhere on Crete, or 174 for information.

Accommodation

This guide recommends a carefully selected cross-section of places to stay, ranging from inexpensive but comfortable hotels to those offering international standards of luxury. However, standards of accommodation are generally quite high, and prices competitive.

Booking a Hotel

- It is quite common to **ask to see a room** before booking it.
- You will need to leave your **passport** at reception to enable registration to be completed and also to act as security against non-payment.
- **Booking ahead** in high season is highly recommended.
- Travelling without pre-booked accommodation is **easier in spring and autumn**. Many hotels close in winter; if travelling between October and April arrange accommodation in advance.
- Many hotels are **family run** and are usually kept spotlessly clean. Facilities may be simple, but there should be everything you need.

Rooms to Rent

- In addition to conventional hotel accommodation, you will also see "**Rooms to rent**" signs (*zimmer* in German and *domatia* in Greek). These will often be spare rooms in private accommodation, and usually very inexpensive. Standards vary so ask to see the room first.
- You may find yourself being made **one of the family**, and be treated to generous Cretan hospitality.

Rates

- All hotels are **inspected annually** by the tourist police, and the room rates and category of hotel agreed. These rates should by law be displayed in each room, usually on the back of the door.
- Out of season it **may be possible to negotiate prices**, but don't expect any leeway in summer. Room rates vary according to the season and according to the standard of the room.
- The **price of breakfast** may or may not be included in the cost of the room, and this will also be indicated in the notice on the door. The quality of hotel breakfasts varies enormously, from the perfunctory to the generous – and usually the cost is the same.

Tips

- If unable to find accommodation yourself, try the **tourist office** (if there is one), any **travel agent**, or ask for the **tourist police**. In some places the latter will have a list of accommodation.
- Many hotels use **solar power** so take your hot shower in the evening as small tanks can sometimes run out of hot water by mid-morning.
- Greek **plumbing systems** are unique. In some places you are not able to flush toilet paper down the toilet as this blocks the pipes. Instead, you use the basket that is provided. The exceptions are modern luxury hotels. If in doubt, ask.

Accommodation Prices
The price of accommodation featured in the guide is indicated below. Prices are for a double room per night.
Inexpensive € under €70 **Moderate** €€ €70–€150 **Expensive** €€€ over €150

Food and Drink

Greek cooking does not have a great reputation but Crete can compete with any Mediterranean island and hold its head high. The Cretan Diet (► 26–27) has been proven to be one of the healthiest in the world, with lots of fresh fish, fruit and vegetables.

Specialities

While similar to conventional Greek cuisine, Crete does have its own specialities, including a good range of local cheeses and wines.

- Try the sweet *mizithra* **cheese** as a change from *feta*.
- **Snails** are quite common on Cretan menus, and have been since Minoan times, while **game** also features.
- **Rabbit** is more popular here than in the rest of Greece, often made into a *stifado* (stew).
- Try *loukaniko*, too (delicious village sausages), **goat** or the local version of *kleftiko* – lamb and cheese in pastry baked in the oven.
- The nearest thing to a national dish is *dakos*, which tastes better than it sounds: a salad of rusks soaked in oil and tossed with tomatoes.

Eating Places

- There is a blurry distinction between **restaurants** and tavernas. Restaurants may be more up-market, and of course there are many smart restaurants in the major towns and tourist resorts. In a restaurant you will probably get a wine glass rather than a little tumbler, and a linen tablecloth instead of the paper variety.
- **Tavernas** are more down to earth, where service will be informal and you may be invited into the kitchen to take a look at the daily specials. The cooking in these family run affairs can be every bit as good as that in pricier places.
- *Psarotavernas* specialise in fish; *psistaries* feature grilled meat, often sold by weight; and *ouzeri* are bars that specialise in ouzo served with the small plates of Greek starters known as *meze* or *mezedes*.
- **Dress code** is smart. Cretans dress up and tourists should do the same.
- You should **book** in the more expensive dining places, especially on Friday and Saturday nights. At casual tavernas simply turn up and hope to be seated. Waiters will ask you to wait till someone has finished.

Eating Times

- **Breakfast** is usually served from an early hour in hotels, but cafés offering breakfast often don't open till about 8am.
- **Lunch** and **dinner** are both eaten late. Cretans have lunch from about 2 or 3pm onwards, although eateries open for business from the tourist trade from about noon onwards. In the evening, in busy resorts, some places may serve food as early as 6pm, but this is only for tourists; in fact some serve all day, so you may not be quite sure if a table of diners is having a very late lunch or an early dinner.
- **Cretans** don't dine in the evening much before 9pm, and truly local restaurants only start buzzing as it gets towards midnight.

The Bill

- Bills often show **two totals**, with and without tax, but naturally you will pay the "with tax" price.
- Most places will have **menus** in Greek and English, and frequently other languages too, especially German.

■ **Service** is usually included but it is common to leave an additional amount of about 5 per cent, or the small change from the bill.

Drinks
■ Do taste the local **barrel wines**, made locally and sold direct from the barrel. The general standard is surprisingly good, although reds tend to fare better than whites.
■ Central Crete and the Sitia region in the east have some of the best **wine-growing areas**.
■ As in the rest of Greece, aniseed flavoured **ouzo** is a popular aperitif.
■ The great Cretan tipple is *rakí*, also known as *tsikoudhia*. It is basically a stronger version of ouzo but without the aniseed taste. A complimentary glass is often served to customers after a meal.

Shopping

Crete is not a destination that attracts people with its shopping, but nevertheless while you are there you will have no trouble finding a good choice of souvenirs for family and friends, as well as gifts for yourself.

This applies whether your taste is for the cheap and cheerful or for more expensive arts and crafts. Note that a lot of the cheap "local" souvenirs are actually made overseas and imported.
 Crete has a wide range of traditional crafts that are kept alive thanks to its popularity as a holiday destination. These include:

Ceramics
■ The familiar cheap and cheerful **blue and yellow plates** of the island are available everywhere.
■ The village of **Margarites** (➤ 142) is the centre for ceramics.

Icons
■ Holy icons are still **made in the traditional way** on Crete (➤ 32–33) but check for the certificate on the back authenticating this.
■ Icons can be found throughout the island in souvenir shops, but the **best quality examples** are to be found at churches and monasteries, and at places such as the Petrakis Icon Workshop in Elounda (➤ 123).

Jewellery
■ All over the island there are jewellery shops selling **fine quality silver and gold**. Pieces are sold by weight and often represent good value.
■ Look for the shops where you can **see the jeweller at work** in the back, then you know you are buying original handcrafted work.

Leatherware
■ Life in the Cretan mountains is tough, and sturdy leatherware has long been made for practical purposes. Today the workshops also produce **handbags, purses, wallets and other items** for the tourist trade, but you can still buy local items such as the long-legged Cretan boots.
■ **Chania** has the widest range (➤ 153).

Weaving
■ This island tradition still flourishes, particularly in mountain towns such as **Kritsa** (➤ 104, 123), **Psychro** (➤ 123) and **Anogia** (➤ 88–89).

- Shop-fronts are festooned with **carpets and rugs**, far too many to have been produced by the one old lady who runs the shop. The better-quality handmade items will invariably be a lot more expensive, but worth it.
- **Chania** is also a good place to buy woven goods (► 153).

Woodcarving

- Many tourist resorts have their own **olive-wood workshop**, with souvenir shops selling attractive carvings of bowls, spoons, salt and pepper sets, plus many other items.

Food and drink

- If you have developed a taste for the local firewater, *rakí*, you might want to take some home. Both *rakí* **and ouzo** can be bought in elegant bottles that could be used afterwards as vases or shelf decorations.
- Almost all towns now have shops specialising in **Cretan herbs and spices**, which the chef of the family will want to investigate.
- **Cretan honey** is popular, being extremely pure and tasty, but is often far more expensive than at home.
- The real bargain is **olive oil**, as Crete produces some of the finest quality oil in Greece.

Entertainment

Arts and Festivals

- Art forms such as **dance and drama** are held all year round; however performances are held much more frequently during summer festivals. At these times, old forts and monuments are turned into theatrical venues. Iraklio (► 70), Chania (► 154), Rethymno (► 154), Sitia (► 124) and Agios Nikolaos (► 124) all have their own local arts festivals.

Bars, Clubs and Discos

- **Bars** are not particularly Cretan, as Greeks are not great drinkers and do most of their socialising in cafés. In recent years, though, fashions have started to change and young Cretans now hang out in stylish bars just like young people the world over. There are plenty of these chic establishments in the main towns, often crowded together in a laneway or a square in the centre of town, or lining the harbout, beach or seaside, and it won't take long to find out where the local action is. Bars in resorts tend to be more tourist-influenced, often modelled on British-style pubs or German *bierkellers*, with big-screen TVs offering MTV or sports channels.
- **Clubs and discos** are usually synonymous, and the larger resorts will normally have a few competing for custom. Some places such as Malia have numerous nightspots thumping out music till the early hours. As with any tourist area, what's fashionable can change from one season to another and clubs, like bars, can change hands, name and style. Some have free entry, others charge an admission fee that buys you your first drink. Prices are not outrageously expensive, and most places don't get going till midnight...and then keep going till the last customers leave. With a lack of listings magazines, look out for flyers on walls and telegraph poles telling you what's on where. Stylish cafés and bars are a good bet for leaflets promoting club nights.

Cinemas

- Cinema-going is a popular pastime on Crete and in many places summer sees the arrival of **open-air cinemas**. These can be great fun, but don't expect to be able to hear every word of the dialogue.

■ Lots of **American films** are shown in their original language with Greek subtitles, but check on the posters around town or at the box office to be sure.

Outdoor Activities

■ **Cycling** and **mountain biking** are not quite as popular as hiking on Crete, but in some resorts it is possible to hire bikes or join a guided tour. Ask at tourist information offices or in local travel agents.

■ **Horse-riding** is a wonderful way of seeing some of Crete's remoter parts. There are several stables around the island, listed in the appropriate section.

■ The best **tennis** courts usually belong to the large resort-hotels. Some are for guests' use only but others will let non-residents play on them for a fee, so it is worth making enquiries. There are public courts in Chania and Iraklio.

■ **Walking** is one of the main reasons many people visit Crete. The mountains are spectacular and unspoilt, but even less energetic visitors feel compelled to take on the challenge of the Samaria Gorge (► 140–141). This trip can easily be arranged from any resort remotely within reach of the gorge. Travel agents will often also offer walking tours to less well-known places, such as the Impros Gorge (► 145), and several towns have specialist walking companies, listed in the text. With a car you can head to the gorges and do the walks independently, though do take note of any weather warnings.

■ **Water sports** are popular throughout the island's resorts and all but the tiniest of places have a water sports centre of some kind. Activities range from banana boats through to jet-skis, water-skiing and scuba diving, although the last is restricted to certain areas due to the fact that there are still many unexplored underwater archaeological sites around Crete. Contact a local diving club for more information; there are several in Chania (► 154), Agios Nikolaos (► 124), Rethymno (► 154) and elsewhere.

Publications

■ The most comprehensive listings of what's going on are to be found in the free *Kriti Times*. Printed in both English and German, it is usually handed out at the airport to new arrivals, but is widely available.

■ **Cretasommer**, also free and printed in English and German, principally features life in Rethymno but includes a few articles on the island generally, too.

Gay and Lesbian Travellers

■ Chania has a **thriving gay scene** with a number of bars and clubs hosting gay events and dance parties although there are no especially gay resorts as there are, say, on Mykonos.

■ **Gay travellers are as welcome** as any other travellers, and Cretans are as tolerant as other Greeks. The more outrageously dressed gay and lesbian couples will probably be looked at with amusement rather than hostility.

■ Be aware of a borderline, though. **Overt behaviour**, which includes public kissing, goes a step too far and may not receive the same amount of tolerance.

■ **Homosexuality is legal** throughout Greece from the age of 17 (male homosexuality is far more common than female), but you will not find many Cretans who flaunt it.

Iraklio

Getting Your Bearings

A graceful Venetian fortress guards the harbour of Crete's capital, Iraklio, the fifth largest city in Greece and the main gateway to the island. Many visitors, however, do no more than make a quick trip to the wonderful Archaeological Museum, or use it as a convenient base for Knossos. But though it's often noisy, busy and clogged with traffic, the city has many charms and a number of excellent restaurants easily repay an overnight stay. The loggia, several churches and the Morosini Fountain are among the attractions that reveal its proud history and character.

Page 45: The Turkish fleet in old Iraklio

Iraklio was heavily bombed during World War II, which accounts for the proliferation of drab, modern concrete buildings in what was formerly a handsome Venetian city. However, a few of the old mansions survive and the old city walls are still intact, running for 3km (2 miles) around the old town and separating it from the sprawling suburbs beyond. Apart from the Natural History Museum, everything of interest in the city lies within the walls. The central thoroughfare through the old town is Odos 25 Avgoustou, which runs from the harbour up past the street market. Most of the main attractions lie along this route, or on small squares near by. Odos Daidalos intersects with Odos 25 Avgoustou and leads to the Archaeological Museum. You can walk the short distance from one sight to another, and there are plenty of cafés and bars to stop at for a cool drink along the way.

Agios Petrou
Dominikanon

Istoriko Mouseio Kritis **3**

Gazi

Gazi

Grevenon

Hanion

Vistaki

Horiatson

GIAMALAKI

Kazantzaki

Kondilaki

Dendidaki   Mihelidaki

KALOKAIRINOU

Agia Ekaterini **4**
Platia
Ag Ekaterinis

Statue in Platia Kornarou

In a Day

If you're not quite sure where to begin your travels, this itinerary recommends a practical and enjoyable day out in Iraklio, taking in some of the best places to see using the Getting Your Bearings map on the previous page. For more information see the main entries.

8:00 am
Get an early start at the ❶ Archaeological Museum (left, ➤ 50–55). If you haven't had breakfast yet, break your visit with a coffee and pastry near by. At the time of writing most of the museum is closed for renovations.

10:30 am
Walk down Odos Daidalos, the main shopping street, and turn right when you reach the end at Platia Venizelou. Continue down Odos 25 Avgoustou, stopping to admire the ❽ Venetian loggia (➤ 63). Just beyond, peek into the lovely ❼ Agios Titos church (➤ 62), set back on a small square. Continue to the end of the street, where it reaches the waterfront.

11:30 am
Walk out along the colourful **harbour** to the ❷ Venetian fortress (below, ➤ 56–57). Be sure to walk beyond the castle to join the locals on their popular walking route along the breakwater.

12:30 pm
Have an early lunch by the waterside at Taverna Paralia (➤ 68), with lovely views of the fortress.

1:30 pm
Walk along the waterfront to the **3 Historical Museum** (left, ➤ 58–59).

3:00 pm
Return to Platia Venizelou and take a closer look at the Morosini Fountain (below). If you've got some time to kill, there's no better spot for people-watching. Have a rest at Bougatsa Kirkor and try Crete's traditional custard pastry, the *bougátsa*, or relax in the nearby El Greco Park.

4:30 pm
Visit the **3 Icon Museum** (➤ 60–61) and the cathedral and Church of Agios Minas (➤ 61), both on the same square. Afterwards, take time for a last look at the Minoan treasures in the Archaeological Museum, or enjoy a pre-dinner drink in one of the bars behind Odos Daidalos (➤ 70).

❶ Archaiologiko Mouseio

Iraklio's Archaeological Museum is not only the major museum on Crete, it is the largest repository of Minoan antiquities anywhere and stands among the finest museums of the ancient world. This magnificent collection of pottery, frescoes, jewellery, ritual objects and utensils brings the Minoan world to life. Come here first, before visiting the ancient palaces and your view of the ruins will be enlivened with a sense of the colour, creativity and richness of the fascinating culture that once flourished on this island.

The collection of the Archaeological Museum covers 5,500 years of Cretan history, from neolithic times (5000–2600 BC) to the end of the Roman era (4th century AD). The original two-storey building was built between 1937 and 1940 but as both the collection and the present-day summer crowds had outgrown the space, major renovations were undertaken to extend and enlarge the building and were underway at the time of research. A new museum is expected to open by 2010.

In the meantime, there is an exhibition of highlights from the museum's collection, displayed in two rooms on the lower floor of the administration building adjoining the original museum (now a construction site). The treasures on display are due to be rotated, but at any one time you're likely to see a selection of pieces from the collection described below. A visit here a must and in some ways it is more pleasurable because you

A procession of figures on the sarcophagus from Agia Triada

TIMELINE
Archaeologists categorise the museum's artefacts into the following periods:
Pre-Palace period: 2600–1900 BC
Old Palace period: 1900–1700 BC
New Palace period: 1700–1450 BC
Late Palace period: 1450–1400 BC
Post-Palace period: 1400–1150 BC
Sub-Minoan, Geometric, Oriental and Archaic periods: 1150–6th century BC
Classical, Hellenistic and Roman periods: 5th century BC–4th century AD

The Phaistos Disc contains many riddles

can take your time enjoying this compact display of archaeological gems.

Buy your tickets (and postcards and museum guide if you choose) at the office at the entrance then proceed down the driveway and around to your right. A guide is not essential, however, as the exhibits are labelled in both Greek and English. The collection is arranged chronologically, with finds from the major Minoan periods grouped according to the sites where they were discovered.

Expect to see some of Crete's oldest artefacts, ranging from neolithic stone tools and crude idols to early Minoan pottery, figurines and jewellery from the Pre-Palace period (see Timeline panel). The ancient bull sports, later an important ritual in palace life, are represented by the small clay figures of bulls with acrobats grasping their horns. Look out, too, for early signs of Minoan craftsmanship in the Vasiliki pottery from eastern Crete, with graceful, elongated spouts and deep red and black mottling obtained by uneven firing. Also noteworthy are the early seal stones (➤ 53).

The greatest highlights, if on display, include finds from Knossos and Malia. Painted and glazed earthenware plaques of the Town Mosaic depict the multistorey dwellings of Minoan architecture. The many human and animal figurines were votive offerings found in peak sanctuaries. Clay *taximata*, representing diseased feet, arms or other parts of the body needing cures, are forerunners of the silver ones pinned to icons in churches today.

Pottery is more elaborate, with the white and red polychrome

EUROPE'S FIRST WRITTEN WORD
The earliest known written history in Europe began on Crete around 2000 BC. Known as Linear A, these inscriptions pre-date the documents of Mycaenean Greece, written in Linear B, by 600 years. Nearly 1,600 Linear A inscriptions have been found to date, and although they are not fully deciphered most are probably administrative records. Only 10 per cent are thought to be religious in nature.

decoration of Kamares ware, and the delicate "egg shell" cups.

The style reaches its height in finds from the same period at Phaistos Palace. Large amphorae sport elaborate spirals, fish and other designs, while a royal banquet set includes a huge fruit stand and a jug with relief decoration of large white flowers. However, the highlight is the Phaistos Disc (➤ 85) with its intricately carved hieroglyphic characters, possibly from a ritual text.

Some of the finest artworks date from the New Palace period when Minoan art reached its peak. These include an exquisite gaming board from Knossos, made of ivory with gold casing and inlaid decoration of rock crystal and lapis lazuli, and two superb statues of the Snake Goddess, sacral relics from the temple repositories. Both figures are bare-breasted, one holding a pair of snakes in her upraised arms, the other with snakes coiled round her outstretched arms. They represent a major Minoan deity, or possibly a priestess engaged in ritual.

A male figurine from the museum's vast collection

Another treasure is the bull's head *rhyton* from Knossos (a *rhyton* is a libation vessel used in religious ceremonies). Magnificently carved from steatite (a black stone), it has inlaid eyes of rock crystal, nostrils of white shell and restored wooden horns.

Other lifelike artworks that are equally impressive include the alabaster head of a lioness, also a libation vessel, from Malia; a stone axe-head carved in the shape of a panther, also from Malia; and the graceful ivory figure of an acrobat in mid-leap. The Jug of Reeds, with its dark colours and patterns

This gold bracelet was a find from Knossos

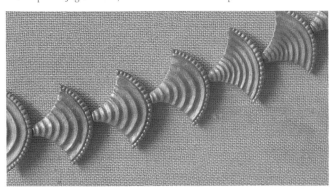

depicting themes from nature, represents new developments in pottery.

Among the Late Palace period finds from the Knossos area is an interesting model of a Minoan house at Archanes and rare examples of Linear A script, the written language of the Minoans, alongside the Linear B script of mainland Greece. Among a range of objects from cemeteries at Knossos and Phaistos is a delightful clay statuette of men locking arms in a ritual dance between the horns of consecration, and another clay scene of ritual washing.

If you're lucky and they have included the following relics among the highlights when you visit, you may also see the bizarre remains of a horse burial, along with a helmet made of boars' tusks, and three enormous bronze double-axes erected on wooden poles that were used to guard the entrance to a room in the old museum.

One exhibit you are sure to be able to appreciate, as it's considered to be one of the museum's greatest treasures, is the most outstanding piece of Minoan jewellery ever found, an intricate honeybee pendant with two gold bees joined round a honeycomb. It should be centre stage among a display of exquisite Minoan jewellery.

Equally famous are three elegantly carved steatite vases from Agia Triada: the harvester vase shows a procession of harvesters and musicians; the chieftain cup portrays an official receiving a tribute of animal skins; and the boxer rhyton depicts boxing, wrestling and bull-leaping.

Below: Allow plenty of time to browse

For many visitors to the Museum, the treasures from the Zakros Palace are pretty special. One of the triumphs of the museum is a stunning rock crystal *rhyton* with a green

MINOAN MOTIFS

Look for the major motifs that appear on artefacts from Minoan times: the double axe, the spiral and the horns of consecration were often painted or etched on pottery, while votive figurines took the shape of bulls, or goddesses with upraised arms.

SMALL IS BEAUTIFUL

Despite their tiny size, seal stones display an amazing degree of craftsmanship. Animals, people, imaginary creatures and hunting or religious scenes were carved in intricate detail on to hard stones such as agate or amethyst. These images were then impressed on to clay seals, which were used as a signature on correspondence or as a guarantee on shipments of goods. No two are alike.

beaded handle, expertly reconstructed from over 300 fragments. The peak sanctuary *rhyton* depicts scenes of Minoan worship.

There should also be finds from settlements in eastern Crete on display, including the site of Gournia, from where there is a marvellous collection of seal stones. The Post-Palace period represents the decline of Minoan art, and the influences of Mycenaean Greece and Egypt. The museum's collection includes dozens of clay sarcophagi (coffins) painted with geometric designs. Many are shaped like bathtubs, and two are complete with skeletons. The magnificent Agia Triada sarcophagus, which survives completely intact, is decorated with elaborate scenes of a funeral procession and an animal sacrifice.

Above; The famous Snake Goddess

The Hall of Frescoes was a highlight of the old museum. Its long corridors were lined with the famous frescoes from Knossos: the bull-leaper, the lily prince, and the dolphins from the queen's bedroom. Only fragments of the original frescoes survive, with the paintings reconstructed around them, but the colour and detail in these few pieces reveal the remarkable skill of these early artists. As did the smaller frescoes, including the sensuous La Parisienne, and the Saffron Gatherer, originally thought to be a boy picking flowers but later reinterpreted as a blue monkey.

The museum also boasted a superb collection of classical Greek and Roman sculpture, which, at the time of research,

PARTING GIFTS

Men were buried with bronze weapons and tools, while bronze mirrors were beloved offerings for female burials.

Right: This clay model shows a typical Minoan house

were on display at the end of the highlights exhibition, and are well worth lingering at before you leave.

TAKING A BREAK

There are many cafés and tavernas nearby on Platia Eleftherias, while the bars and cafés of Odos Korai are also a short walk away.

➕ 183 D4 ✉ Odos Xanthoudidou 1 ☎ 2810-226092 🕐 Mon 12–5, Tue–Sun and holidays 8–5; reduced hours in winter 🍴 Cafés nearby (€) 🚌 Bus stop near museum 💷 Expensive ❓ No flash photography

---

ARCHAEOLOGICAL MUSEUM: INSIDE INFO

Top tips Visit first thing in the morning, during lunchtime or in the late afternoon to **avoid the worst of the coach-party crowds.**
■ While the old museum was enormous and could be overwhelming, in its current temporary location, the highlights exhibition takes just an hour or so to see.

Must sees
■ Phaistos Disc
■ Bull's Head Rhyton
■ Hall of the Frescoes
■ Snake Goddesses
■ Rock Crystal Rhyton

Hidden gems
Don't overlook the tiny gems, such as the seal stones, the honeybee pendant, or the ivory butterfly.

One to miss The classical Greek and Roman statues seem anticlimactic after the Minoan art.

2 Enetiko Limani & Frourio Koules

Iraklio's Venetian harbour is one of its most attractive features, and a stroll around here with a visit to the Venetian fortress that guards it is a relaxing treat. From the fortress you get an excellent view, not only of the city but of the remains of the Venetian shipyards, or *arsenali*, across the water.

Arsenali

Close up, the *arsenali* are none too impressive, surrounded as they now are by the modern city, but the view from the fortress shows something of their old scale and style. A look at the model in the Historical Museum (▶ 58–59) also helps re-create a picture of what life must have been like under Venetian rule. These 16th-century shipyards would have resounded to the noise of large boats being built and repaired, where today it is the bobbing of the small boats belonging to Iraklio's fishermen that sets the tone.

The Fortress

The fortress, which dominates the harbour entrance, was built between 1523 and 1540, though there had been several earlier forts on the site, one of which was destroyed in an earthquake in 1303. The Venetians rebuilt it and named it Rocca al Mare, Rock in the Sea, and the impressive name is appropriate for the building you discover beyond the entrance gate.

ST MARK'S LION

The winged lion of St Mark the Evangelist was the emblem of the Venetian Republic. It was depicted in all areas under the Republic's dominion, carved in limestone or marble above gateways or on public buildings and fortifications. Some 80 reliefs have been recorded on Crete.

ENETIKO LIMANI & FROURIO KOULES: INSIDE INFO

Top tip Locals stroll and ride bicycles by here and then along the breakwater.
■ Fishermen also mend their nets on their boats and on the dock.

Hidden gems Look for the **lions of St Mark** (see panel) above the entrance gate and on the seaward wall.

Top left: The graceful arches of Iraklio's *arsenali*

Inside, you step into a huge dark vaulted room with various rooms and passageways leading off it. Ahead and to the right is a long steep slope that leads to the upper levels, where you can climb the walls for fine views of the harbour and city beyond, or out to sea. Some of the towers can be climbed, too.

While here, mull over the most significant episode in the history of the fortress. In 1647 the Venetian rulers of Crete retreated into the fortress under siege from Turkish invaders. That siege was to last until 1669 and so became one of the longest in history. Eventually the Venetians had to succumb, but only after a long and bloody struggle during which it is said that 30,000 Venetians and 118,000 Turks lost their lives.

Above: Today the Venetian fortress guards only the fishermen's boats

The fortress has been extensively refurbished and some say it now looks more like a film set, but its scale remains impressive. It houses temporary exhibitions, and occasional plays and concerts are performed in the upper level.

TAKING A BREAK

You can enjoy good views of the fortress over a drink or a meal at the **Taverna Paralia** (➤ 68).

Left: The Lion of St Mark, on the fortress walls

Venetian Fortress
✚ 179 E5
🖐 Inexpensive ❓ Photography allowed

❸ Istoriko Mouseio Kritis

For an overview of the history of both Crete and Iraklio, a visit to the small but informative History Museum occupying an elegant Venetian town house is a must. Highlights of the collection include the study of Nikos Kazantzakis and the only work by El Greco still on the artist's native island.

At the ticket desk be sure to pick up one of the leaflets, available in Greek, English or German, which gives a map of the museum and a brief note of what is in each room. Most of the displays have information in both Greek and English, but in some instances the details given are fairly basic.

That said, in **Room I**, to your right as you enter, the information panels are anything but basic. They cover in some detail four of the major periods in Crete's history and correspond to four shelves of objects from those periods: the First Byzantine (330–824), the Arab occupation (824–961), the Second Byzantine (961–1204) and Venetian rule (1204–1669).

Forming the major display in this room is a wonderful 1:500 scale model of Iraklio as it was in 1645. At that time it was still known as Chandax, the name given to the city by the Arabs when they made it the island capital in the early 9th century; it may derive from the Arabic words *Rabdh el-Khandak* (Fortress of the Moat). On the walls beside it maps show the development of the city over the years; note the buttons beneath the displays that illuminate the relevant parts of the model.

The museum tour continues beyond the ticket desk, with the rooms spread over several levels.

Room II is the Ceramics Room and has beautiful bowls and plates imported from Italy during the Venetian period. These are cleverly displayed side by side with locally made pottery from the same period, clearly showing the Italian influence on local designs. Lovely, delicate jugs and bowls from the Arab occupation of the island are also on display.

The rest of the ground floor has several rooms containing Byzantine items, Venetian coats of arms and carvings (note the

A typical Cretan house, displayed in the Historical Museum

Manolis Kazanis, Cretan revolutionary leader

fountain from a 17th-century palazzo in Room VI), with stairs leading up to the second level.

The highlight of **Level B** is undoubtedly the small, dimly lit room containing El Greco's painting of the *Monastery of St Catherine Beneath Mount Sinai*. This, his only work to remain on Crete, was painted in 1570. Some background to it is given. Elsewhere on this floor are several icons, and at the rear one room is given over to the struggle for independence against the Turks.

The major display on **Level C** comprises the writer Nikos Kazantzakis's study when he lived in Antibes from 1948 to 1957, complete with manuscripts of his works, his library of books, and copies of his own books translated into many languages. It's an essential visit for anyone interested in this author. The top floor of the museum contains a folklore collection based on the theme of the life cycle of birth, marriage and death. The museum's fine collections of weavings, embroidery, old costumes, household items, musical instruments and many other objects contribute to the display, along with newly acquired pieces.

TAKING A BREAK

There are several excellent tavernas close to here, but take a two-minute stroll towards the harbour to enjoy a drink or a meal at the **Taverna Kastella** overlooking the water.

Wall-painting showing the Turkish fleet in the harbour at Iraklio

🔳 179 D4 ✉ Odos Lysimahou Kalokerinou 7 and corner of 27 Odos Sofokoli Venezelou ☎ 2810-283219/288708; www.historical-museum.gr 🕐 Apr–Oct Mon–Sat 9–5 💷 Expensive ❓ No flash photography

HISTORICAL MUSEUM: INSIDE INFO

Must see El Greco's painting *Monastery of St Catherine Beneath Mount Sinai*.

Hidden gems Cabinets in the centre of Room I, slightly overshadowed by the other displays, contain **fascinating glass and clay hand grenades** found on a galleon that sank in 1669.

One to miss The **Emmanuel Tsouderos room**, opposite the Nikos Kazantzakis room, is unlikely to appeal unless you have a deep interest in Greek politics.

❹ Agia Ekaterini

Cretan icon painters were considered to be the best in the world, and here in the small Church of Agia Ekaterini you can see some of the finest works by one of the greatest masters of the art, Michael Damaskinos. In addition, this excellent collection includes religious vestments, bibles, illuminated manuscripts, coins and frescoes rescued from or donated by churches and monasteries all over Crete.

The church that houses the collection was built in 1555, but the seating has been removed to expose the marble floors and provide space for the display cabinets in the aisles and around the sides. Icons grace the walls.

Detail from a work by Michael Damaskinos

Just inside the door is the ticket desk, with six hugely impressive 16th-century icons, the work of Michael Damaskinos, hanging on the wall opposite. He was the only Cretan painter of his era to rival the talents of El Greco himself. Like the master, Damaskinos went to Venice to study, but he returned to his native island and the icons here are considered to be among his finest works. Depicting various

AGIA EKATERINI: INSIDE INFO

Top tips The museum's **opening hours do change** from time to time, so check with the tourist office in advance if you can.

■ With **no air-conditioning**, the building can get very hot and stuffy, so visit early in the day if possible.

Hidden gem In what would be the south chapel of the church, look for the exceptional icon of the **Lady of the Kardiotissa** from Moni Kera. The Virgin, dressed in red, has sorrowful eyes that seem to stare right into your soul.

biblical events such as the *Adoration of the Magi*, the *Last Supper* and the *Burning Bush*, they were all painted in between 1582 and 1591 for Moni Vrontisiou (Vrontisiou Monastery) northwest of Zaros (➤ 156–157). Their liveliness and depth of image and colour make them seem as if they were done yesterday. They were brought to Iraklio in 1800 to save them from destruction by the Turks.

Other Byzantine Treasures

In the central aisle two cases contain Byzantine coins and holy manuscripts. On the left aisle is a series of large icons saved from mountain chapels and monasteries; they mostly date from the 15th and 16th centuries and are anonymous. Note the nearby case of lovely 16th-century illuminated manuscripts from Moni Epanosiphi and, opposite these, the ornately carved wooden bishop's throne from Moni Kera.

You'll see more icons as you approach the high altar, including a very vivid 17th-century *Last Judgement* in which naked souls are cast down into hell where they are being eagerly greeted by devils throwing them into the fiery furnace.

Round to the left of the altar the collection broadens out to include brightly coloured frescoes and a large stone iconostasis. Two cases contain chalices, bible covers and a holy cross.

On leaving the church, walk across the square to see the small **Church of Agios Minas**, if open, and the large 19th-century cathedral of the same name with its elaborate metal chandeliers, beautiful painted ceilings and vast stone pulpit.

TAKING A BREAK

Walk along Odos Karterou at the southeast corner of the square to bring you to **Platia Kornarou** (➤ 64), where the Turkish well house now serves as a charming café.

🕂 183 D3 ⊠ Platia Agia Aikaterinis 🕘 Mon–Fri 10–1 💰 Inexpensive ❓ No photography

At Your Leisure

5 Mouseio Fisikis Istorias Kritis

It's well worth visiting the Natural History Museum, housed in a modern air-conditioned building outside the city walls at the University of Crete on the Knossos road, with additional exhibition halls west of Iraklio. The museum provides a wonderful introduction to the wildlife, plants and natural environment of Crete, and if you are planning trips to the countryside or a drive around the island, it will certainly enhance your appreciation of the things you'll see. It lies about halfway between the town centre and Knossos, so you can easily stop off on your way to or from the Minoan palace. Look for the colourful banners waving outside.

The ground-floor rooms contain informative displays on the flora and fauna of Crete. Life-size dioramas re-create cave, forest, wetland and shoreline environments, and show the birds and animals that inhabit them. Both native birds of prey and migrating species are highlighted. Glass cases in the gift shop house live snakes, the curious ocellated skink and the Cretan spiny mouse. Other rooms are devoted to endangered species and to creatures of the high mountains, including the Cretan wild goat (*kri-kri*) and the magnificent griffon and lammergeier vultures.

To reach the upper level you walk through a lovely botanical garden,

Platia Eleftherias – "Liberty Square"

especially aromatic in spring and summer when the many species of wild herbs are in bloom. Upstairs is an informative exhibit on the evolution of mankind, a re-created Minoan farm, and displays of fossils, rocks and minerals that illustrate Crete's geological evolution.

➕ Off map at 179 E1 ✉ Odos Knosou 157 and Odos Sofokli Venezelou ☎ 2810-324661/282740; www.nhmc.uoc.gr ⏱ Mon–Fri 8:30–2:30, Sun 10–3 🍴 Coffee shop (€) 🚌 2, 3, 4 💰 Moderate ❓ Photography allowed

6 Platia Eleftherias

Its name means "Liberty Square", and this large open space at the top of Odos Daidalos, opposite the Archaeological Museum, provides freedom from the sometimes claustrophobic feel of the city. This square was the centre of the city, and though the ring of rushing traffic around the edge has somewhat dampened its appeal, locals still frequent it for an evening stroll. There are benches beneath the trees, and and restaurants alongside.

➕ 179 E3

7 Agios Titos

Agios Titos sits back from the main road on a lovely square. With its sky-blue ceiling and dome, triple-tiered carved wooden chandelier and modern stained-glass windows, it has a light, airy feel in contrast to most of the churches you'll visit on the island. Built during the Second Byzantine period (➤ 17, 18), it

The lovely façade of Agios Titos

armoury and now houses the town hall. It stands opposite the Morosini Fountain (see Platia Venizelou ➤ 64).
⊕ 179 D3

The elegant Venetian loggia

was the seat of the Metropolitan (bishop) of Crete. During the Turkish occupation it was converted into a mosque but was rebuilt following an earthquake in 1856.

When the Turkish population left Crete in 1923 it was reconsecrated to St Titus, Crete's first bishop. His remains had been kept here for 700 years until the Venetians took them to Venice in 1669. They were returned in 1966, and the saint's skull now lies in a gold reliquary.
⊕ 179 E4 ✉ Odos 25 Avgoustou
🕑 Generally mornings and evenings ✋ Free

🖐 Enotiki Loggia

After the fortress, this is Iraklio's second most handsome building. Built in the 1620s by Francisco Morossni, it was a place of meeting and recreation for the Venetian nobility. Its Palladian style combines Doric order on the lower floor with Ionic on the upper. Medallions of famous Cretans decorate the ground-floor porch, with its elegant arches. The loggia forms part of a larger building that once held the Venetian

🖐 Agios Markos

The Church of Agios Markos (St Mark), first built in 1239, was the church of the duke, ruler of the island. It became a cathedral in Venetian times but, like most other Iraklio churches, was converted by the Turks into a mosque. Unlike the others, however, it was not reconsecrated after their departure

and in 1923 it became the National Bank. Now restored, with a striking colonnaded porch and marble doorway, it is used as a concert hall and art gallery. The arched ceiling, fat pillars and stone walls of the interior make a superb display space for exhibitions of contemporary art.

➕ 179 D3 ✉ Odos 25 Avgoustou ⊘ No set times, but generally evenings 🎟 Free

🔟 Platia Venizelou

This small central square is one of the liveliest in the capital and a popular focal point for tourists and locals alike. It is named for the great Cretan statesman Elefthérios Venizélos, who became prime minister of Greece. Also known as Lion Square or Fountain Square, its centrepiece is the Morosini Fountain. Francisco Morosini, the Venetian governor of the city, built this regal work in 1628. An aqueduct, 16km (10 miles) long, was constructed to bring water down from the mountains. The four stone lions supporting the central basin have great character and are even older; dating from the 14th century, they are thought to have come from another fountain. Carvings of mermaids, tritons and other marine figures decorate the curvaceous marble base.

The square has plenty of cafés and restaurants where you can have a coffee, an ice cream or the custard-

The former church of Agios Markos

filled Cretan speciality, *bougátsa*. It's a perfect vantage point on the passing scene, but if you prefer a quieter retreat try the nearby El Greco Park. It has pretty gardens and a children's playground at one end.

➕ 179 D3

FOR CHILDREN

Venetian Harbour and Fortress (▶ 56–57)
El Greco Park (▶ above)
Natural History Museum (▶ 62)
A ride on the **Happy Train**, which follows the Venetian wall around the old city. Departures from the Archaeological Museum on the hour, 11am–2pm, and from the Venetian Harbour April–October 6–9pm; buy tickets on board (tel: 6897-33624).

🔟 Platia Kornarou

Iraklio's lively street market ends at Platia Kornarou, a small square that makes a pleasant place to rest awhile. The stone kiosk in the centre, which once housed a Turkish fountain, has been converted into a small café. Beside it is the Bembo Fountain, named after the Venetian commander, who first supplied the town with running water. It was erected in 1588 and incorporates the torso of a Roman statue from Ierapetra (▶ 116), about 65km (40 miles) southeast of Iraklio.

➕ 179 D2

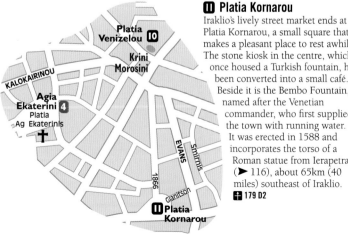

Where to... Stay

Prices

Prices are for a double room per night in high season including taxes

€ under €70   €€ €70–€150   €€€ over €150

Atlantis Hotel €€€

This is a decent hotel in the centre of town, and though it has some 160 rooms and suites you would still be advised to book ahead in summer as it is popular with tour groups and business conferences. Some rooms have views over the harbour, so ask if one of these is available when you book. Not far from the Archaeological Museum and only a short walk to most other city attractions, the Atlantis has so many of its own facilities that you hardly need to leave it: gym, pool, laundry, bars, restaurant, shops and even a rooftop garden.

➕ 183 F4 ✉ Ygias 2 ☎ 2810-229103; www.theatlantishotel.gr

Capsis Astoria €€€

Although right on Iraklio's main square, the Capsis is quiet inside and offers comfortable, reasonably priced accommodation. All the rooms, bright and modern , have been renovated and feature lots of wood furnishings, have plenty of closet space, TV, phone, mini-bar, air-conditioning and ensuite facilities (baths not showers).
The terrific rooftop pool has its own bar, and there are great views over the city. It stays open till 10pm and is a very popular spot for an evening swim.

➕ 179 E3 ✉ Platia Eleftherias 11 ☎ 2810-343080/2; www.capsishotel.gr

El Greco Hotel €

Better than average for a moderately priced hotel, the El Greco is in the heart of the city, close by the busy market and the characterful Platia Venizelou (▶ 64). Its 90 plain but pleasant and clean rooms are all ensuite with phone and heating. Most have balconies, TVs and air-conditioning (costs an extra €7 per day), so if you are staying in high season try to book one of these. The bar/breakfast room, spacious lobby and friendly staff all add to the relaxed atmosphere.

➕ 179 D3 ✉ Odos 1821 4 ☎ 2810-28107i; www.elgrecohotel.gr

Galaxy Hotel €€€

After a much-needed facelift, the Galaxy is looking rather swish. Situated slightly out of the centre, about a kilometre along the road to Knossos, the hotel is within reach of the city sights and buses stop outside for those without a car. Rooms are comfortable and well-equipped, and there's every amenity you can think of, including restaurants, bars, shops, a sauna, and big swimming pool, making this an excellent choice for families in summer.

➕ 183 F4 ✉ Leoforos Dimokratias 75 ☎ 0810-238812; www.galaxy-hotel.com/gr

Hotel Kronos €

This clean, friendly, inexpensive hotel stands right on the waterfront road, which does mean some traffic noise at night in the front rooms. That aside, it offers good value accommodation in the centre of town. Downstairs is a lounge doubles as the breakfast room, and there is a bar with a soft-drinks cabinet. The 32 rooms are a good size and have everything needed for a comfortable stay: balconies, phone, TV, ensuite facilities.

➕ 179 D4 ✉ Odos Sofokli Venizelou 2, Agarathou ☎ 2810-28240; www.kronoshotel.gr

Lato Hotel €€

In an excellent location overlooking the Venetian harbour and a short stroll from the city centre and museums, the Lato is one of the most welcoming hotels in Iraklio. It's also one of the most stylish, with a chic contemporary interior that extends to the light-filled breakfast room and dazzlingly dark restaurant. Each of the individually designed rooms is very smart (some come with funky cow-skin rugs) and all have TV, mini-bar, and air-conditioning/heating. Ask for one with harbour views. Drivers will appreciate the tiny car park.

☩ **183 F4**
✉ **Odos Epimenidou 15**
☎ **2810-228103**

Marin Dream Hotel €€

After a recent renovation, the Marin Dream is now a rather stylish hotel. In a handy location near the harbour and port, it's also within walking distance of shops, restaurants and sights. The

well-equipped rooms have clean contemporary look, and all the mod cons you'd expect of this standard, while some have superb harbour vistas. Car parking is a 5-minute walk away, by the harbour.

☩ **183 F4** ✉ **Doukos Mpofor 12** ☎ **28103-00018; www.marinhotel.gr**

AROUND IRAKLIO

Apollonia Beach Hotel €€€

Standing just 10km west of the centre of Iraklio, the luxury Apollonia has its own beach and the local bus stops right outside the entrance. The 321 rooms, bungalows and suites, all with either a balcony or terrace, are spread around the large gardens and there are two outdoor pools, a children's pool and a heated indoor pool, as well as numerous sports facilities including water sports, cycling and horse-riding. With two pools, it's also ideal for children of all ages.

☩ **183 F4** ✉ **Amoudara** ☎ **2810-821602/821624; www.apollonia.gr** ☀ **Apr–Oct**

Candia Maris €€€

About 6km (4 miles) west of the city centre but with a quick and regular bus service into Iraklio, the Candia Maris makes an ideal base if you want to explore the city but also enjoy the beach. Fully renovated, its excellent facilities include a fitness centre, tennis and squash courts, three swimming pools (plus one for children), water sports, an indoor games room, three restaurants and four bars. The rooms are spacious and bright.

☩ **183 F4** ✉ **Amoudara** ☎ **2810-377000; www.maris.gr/candia** ☀ **Mar–Nov**

Grecotel Amirandes €€€

A contemporary interpretation of a grand Minoan Palace, with elegant, white, cube-like buildings, wooden pillars, and tall palm trees, this luxurious new resort is Crete's most breathtaking. It's also the island's most romantic, set right on the sea and surrounded by still ponds and swimming pools, serenely lit by night. Rooms are luxuriously

furnished and equipped with all the amenities you'd expect. The hotel has myriad restaurants and bars, specialising in everything from Cretan to Asian cuisine, so you never have to leave, and while it's only 20 minutes east of Iraklio, it's very tempting not to.

☩ **184 B4** ✉ **Gouves, Iraklio area** ☎ **28970-41103; www.grecotel.com/crete/amirandes/**

Minoa Palace €€

The 4-star Minoa Palace offers a very reasonable room rate. Half-board and full-board options are available. All rooms have balconies with sea views, and the hotel boasts its own private beach as well as two pools. Sports facilities include tennis courts and horse-riding. Close to the airport, it would make a good base for the first or last night's stay. A car is advisable, though there is a public bus service into Iraklio, 6km (4 miles) west.

☩ **184 A4** ✉ **Amnissos Beach** ☎ **2810-380404; www.akshotels.com** ☀ **Apr–Oct**

Where to...
Eat and Drink

IRAKLIO

Brillant €€€

Iraklio's most fashionable restaurant is the place to head for special night out. The strikingly elegant room is particularly moody at night and the service is warmer than you'd expect from such a hip eatery. The food shines as much as the design, so if you have time opt for the *degustation* menu, order some fine Cretan wines, and let the chef impress you with his creative combinations of seasonal Mediterranean products. On weekends Brillant fills late with dressed-up locals, so book a table for 10pm to enjoy the atmosphere.

➕ 183 F4 ☒ Lato Hotel, Odos Epimenidou 15 ☎ 28103-34459; www.brillantrestaurant.gr
🕐 Daily, lunch and dinner

Giovanni's €€€

Despite the Italian name, this up-market restaurant has a very Greek menu. A speciality of the house is feta cheese baked in the oven with olive oil, tomato and oregano, but a mixed seafood platter also features regularly, as does fresh fish – which can be expensive. Outdoor and indoor seating, a good Greek wine list and a generally smart look tend to attract a well-to-do Iraklio crowd.

➕ 183 F4 ☒ Odos Korai 12 ☎ 2810-246338 🕐 Mon–Sat 12:30pm–2am, Sun 5pm–1:30am

La Grande Trattoria €€–€€€

Despite its smart appearance with candle-lit tables on two floors, this Italian restaurant in the heart of the nightlife district has something for everyone. The extensive menus range from pizzas and pastas to house specialities featuring chicken, fish and veal. Many of the dishes have an international flair using creative combinations of ingredients that go beyond the usual Italian fare and the trattoria claims to have Iraklio's only singing chef.

➕ 183 F4 ☒ Odos Korai 6 ☎ 2810-300225 🕐 Daily noon–3pm, 5pm–late

Ionia €€

Founded in 1923, when it played host to the archaeologists from Knosos, the Ionia claims to be the oldest restaurant on Crete. There are a few seats outside but most are indoors in a fairly nondescript modern room decorated with old archaeological photos on the walls. Filled more with Greeks than with tourists, it serves up excellent home-cooked dishes such as grilled chicken, grilled lamb chops and sardines. "Whatever is fresh in the market," says the manager, "that is what we cook. Seasonal food."

➕ 179 D3 ☒ Odos Evans 3 ☎ 2810-283213
🕐 Mon–Fri 8am–10:30pm, Sat 8am–4pm

Ligo Krasi, Ligo Thalassa €

This simple no-nonsense taverna with enormous glass windows overlooking the harbour may not be Iraklio's most attractive eatery, but it's one of the city's most popular. It makes up for a lack of looks with exceedingly generous portions of *mezedes* – the speciality being freshly caught and freshly cooked seafood – at unbelievably low prices. The place is packed throughout the day and night with locals, so service can be harried and staff may be abrupt, but they're efficient and if you compliment their food you'll definitely get a smile.

➕ 183 F4 ⊠ Corner I. Mitsotaki & Marineli (opposite Venetian Harbour) ☎ 28103-00501 ⏱ Daily, all day

Loukoulos €€€

With its lovely courtyard beneath a spreading lemon tree and bougainvillea, and views into the kitchen, this stylish restaurant offers the very best Greek and Italian cuisine, with other flourishes too. The wine list is excellent and the service, by knowledgeable staff who can describe each dish in mouthwatering detail, impeccable. One superb speciality is veal with a sauce of dried figs.

➕ 183 F4 ⊠ Odos Korai 5 ☎ 2810-224435 ⏱ Mon–Sat noon–1am, Sun 6:30pm–midnight

Odos Aigaiou €€

With a rather smart dining room inside graced by big picture windows, and an expansive terrace outside overlooking the port, this is a reliable year-round restaurant choice for a long lazy meal. The speciality is superb fresh seafood and the fish and lobster (when in season) are recommended. Choose the seafood from the display counter and they'll cook it to order. The menu includes traditional Greek dishes and pastas.

➕ 183 F4 ⊠ Odos Aigaiou & Spanaki (opposite port) ☎ 28102-41410; www.odosaigaiou.gr ⏱ Daily, all day

O Kyriakos €€€

The Kyriakos has been around for 50 years and is where visiting dignitaries tend to be taken. There is a relaxed outdoor seating area shielded from the street by lots of greenery, and a slightly more formal dining room inside with white walls and yet more plants. Service is very friendly and the restaurant prides itself on its range of good *meze*. Aubergines stuffed with feta is a simple dish but deliciously done.

➕ 183 F4 ⊠ Odos Leoforos Dimokratias 53 ☎ 2810-224649 ⏱ Daily noon–5, 7–1am

Pantheon €€

With outdoor seating on both sides of the covered side street, the Pantheon couldn't be closer to the butchers and the greengrocers of Iraklio's market. It serves plenty of conventional dishes such as chicken and moussaka, but take a look in the kitchen to see the day's more unusual specials, such as lamb cooked in a clay pot in the oven with artichokes and peas, or aubergine stuffed with lamb and topped with cheese.

➕ 183 F4 ⊠ Odos Theodosaki 2 ☎ 2810-241652 ⏱ Mon–Sat 11am–11pm

Syntages €€

In a handsome, blue and white painted, neo-classical house, in street behind Eleftherias Square, this elegant restaurant quickly became a local favourite only short time after opening. You can sit downstairs in the tiled courtyard or the informal interior or upstairs in a slightly more elegant dining room. The décor features quirky touches such as handwriting on the walls, yet the focus is firmly on the outstanding Mediterranean food, from traditional home-style cooking to more refined dishes executed with creative flair.

➕ 183 F4 ⊠ Odos Koziri 3 ☎ 28102-41378 ⏱ Mon–Sat 1pm–midnight, Sun 1pm–5pm

Taverna Paralia €

Set right on the waterfront, the Paralia's tables look out over the occasionally crashing waves and across to the Venetian fortress. On breezy days you can choose the sheltered seating indoors, where the style is typically Greek – blue and white décor with checked tablecloths. The menu includes many standard Greek dishes, plus pasta and pizza, but the speciality is fresh fish such as swordfish or sea bream, simply grilled.

➕ 183 F4 ⊠ Odos Venizelou 5 ☎ 2810-282475 ⏱ Apr–Oct daily 10am–midnight

Where to... Shop

Like any major city, Crete's capital has no shortage of shops. Most cater for the locals so if you're after traditional crafts you'll find more choice elsewhere on the island. That said, Iraklio can offer a selection of all Crete's popular souvenirs.

Odos Daidalos, a pedestrianised thoroughfare, is the main tourist shopping street. These days it's mainly given over to fashion, with names such as Hugo Boss, Zara for men and women, Timberland, Nautica, and some shoe shops. The more touristy shops are towards the top end of the street, approaching the Archaeological Museum.

For unique Cretan gifts, try **Galerie Dedalou** at No 11, where you'll find replica coins and Byzantine crosses, repro watches, jewellery, silverware, icons and worry beads.

Aerakis, at No 35, specialises in contemporary and traditional Greek music; also on this street are **Virgin Records** and **Metropolis**, for international artists.

In Iraklio you are especially likely to see gold and silver jewellery with Minoan motifs, or replicas of famous pieces such as the honeybee pendant from the museum. Shops opposite the Archaeological Museum have a fine selection.

You could also try **Vassilakis** at 28 Odos 25 Avgoustou, a family-run shop with good prices. **Kassotakis** jewellery workshop, 14 Odos Katechaki, specialises in historically inspired Byzantine and archaic jewellery.

The square opposite the Archaeological Museum is lined with shops catering for tourists, with pottery, statues, icons, decorative Cretan daggers and replicas of the Phaistos Disc and other Minoan treasures. There are also many rugs, textiles and woven goods, but these are often imported or factory made. True handmade goods will have rough stitching on the back and are more expensive.

Although **Odos 25 Avgoustou** is mainly flanked with travel agents and car-hire companies, there are a few shops worth browsing for gifts. **Emika**, at No 15, has a good selection of wines from local wine co-operatives as well as gift bottles of ouzo, herbed olive oils in pretty bottles, Cretan honey and packets of herbs. Further up the street, next to the loggia, **Cretan Nature** has a similar selection of gift items, including olive-oil soap and creams.

The most colourful place to shop is the market (open weekdays) on **Odos 1866**, also known as Market Street, which is always packed with both locals and tourists. There are stalls selling fresh fruit and vegetables, honey, olives, spices, nuts, dried fruit and sweets, bakers, and butchers with skinned lambs and rabbits. Cheese shops will let you sample cheeses from different villages before you buy. This is the place to find Cretan wedding loaves – the wreath-like bread topped with flower decoration – for a kitchen ornament. One shop sells lace tablecloths and embroidered linens, and you can also buy sponges, T-shirts, leather bags, belts and sandals.

There is also a large market on Saturday morning near the bus station, opposite the port.

Odos Chandakos, behind Platia Venizelou, has some nice little shops with handcrafted jewellery and other gifts.

Busy **Odos Kalokairinou** is Iraklio's high street, with chain stores and other fashion and shoe shops. There are also shops selling embroidered goods along this street.

Where to...
Be Entertained

Nightlife in Iraklio is generally not the raucous affair you find in the beach party towns. If that's what you're after, head for the clubs along the coastal strip at Amoudara, west of the city, the hottest club scene in summer, or to Chersonisou or Malia (▶ 124) to the east. Also note that while bars are open all day until late, clubs and discos don't start up until 11pm or midnight.

NIGHTCLUBS

Nightclubs in town are geared for the locals, and it can be hard to find the "right" one unless you go with someone who knows the scene. Many are around the harbour, such as 4 U Club and Galea behind the port promenade. Two long-time favourites on Odos Bofor are Yacht Club and Privilege.

BARS

The Platia Venizelou cafés are ideal for people watching and make an excellent coffee stop while a pastry at the Bougatsa café opposite the Lion Fountain is a must. Off Daidalos, Odos Ioannou Perthikari leads to Korai, Iraklio's most happening streets and the heart of its nightlife. By day, locals relax at the chic cafés and bars; by night the lanes are crammed with young hipsters sipping cocktails. Each season the bars get makeovers and name changes, so just head to the one you like the look of. The bars on Odos Chandakos, running south of Platia Venizelou, see a more down-to-earth crowd at their terrace tables.

TRADITIONAL MUSIC

During high season many restaurants hold tourist-orientated "Greek nights" with traditional music and dancing. For more authentic experience, head to the small backstreet ouzeris and tavernas where locals go. Look for musical instrument painted on the sign, indicating that there'll be live music at some point in the night.

ARTS FESTIVAL

Iraklio's summer arts festival is held from late June to mid-September and features Greek and international artists in music, dance and theatre productions that range from ballet to Greek drama. Performances take place on the roof of the Venetian fort or in the Nikos Kazantzakis Open-Air Theatre at Jesus Bastion (tel: 2810-242977, box office). In summer the latter is also used as an open-air cinema. In the town centre, the Alpha Odeon cinema at Platia Eleftherias shows English films with Greek subtitles.

INTERNET CAFÉS

Good central internet cafés include Sportcafé, off Odos 25 Avgoustou on Kosma Zotou; Netclub and Mitsotaki 2, near the waterfront; and GG at Odos Korai 6.

SPORTS

Most sports facilities are located out of town. To find a good tennis court, contact the Tennis Club of Iraklio at Odos Bofor 17 (tel: 2810-344545).

The Mountaineering and Skiing Club of Irakleion organises weekend excursions. Visitors are welcome (tel: 2810-227609).

Central Crete

Getting Your Bearings

Visitors who fly into Iraklio and then head east or west along the coast in search of sandy beaches often overlook central Crete. But turn south instead and you'll find mountains, caves, gorges, monasteries and churches, craft villages and hill villages, Minoan sites and, at the end of your journey, beautiful beach resorts like Matala and Agia Galini.

Central Crete claims the top attraction on the island, the ruins of ancient Knossos, but it also has smaller, equally fascinating sites. Phaistos, near the south coast, has an attractive setting overlooking the Mesara Plain. Here you can see the spot where archaeologists found what is perhaps the island's single most important historical item: the Phaistos Disc.

Those fascinated by history will also revel in two other sites close to Phaistos. One is the Roman site at Gortys, the other the Minoan villa of Agia Triada. Both gloriously demonstrate that small can be beautiful, their human scale really bringing history alive.

The mountain village of Zaros is a gateway to some wonderful walking, but central Crete is also ideal for those who want to combine history with sunbathing. The south coast resorts of Matala and Agia Galini both have good beaches, good eating and nightlife, and make great bases for exploring the whole area. From south to north is little more than an hour's drive…or more like a week if you want to explore every nook and cranny.

Making sense of Agia Triada

★ Don't Miss

1. **Knossos** ➤ 76
2. **Gortys** ➤ 81
3. **Phaistos** ➤ 84

At Your Leisure

4. Arolithos ➤ 87
5. Tilisos ➤ 87
6. Agioi Deka ➤ 87
7. Fodele ➤ 88
8. Anogia ➤ 88
9. Oros Psiloritis & Ideon Andron ➤ 89
10. Mouseio Kritikis Ethnologias ➤ 90
11. Agia Triada ➤ 90
12. Matala ➤ 91
13. Agia Galini ➤ 91

0 10 km
0 5 miles
Sises
7 Fodele
Kolpos
Irakliou
Doxarou
Iraklio
Arolithos 4
Tilisos 5
Knossos 1
Zoniana
8 Anogia
1575m
Sitaras
1199m
Voskero
Voutes
Idi (Psiloritis)
Oros
Psiloritis 9
Pano
Arhanes
Fourfouras
9 Ideon Andron
Dafnes
Prof
Ilias
Kato Asites
1920m
Alikadam
Kamares
Zaros
Gergeri
Ag Varvara
Melampes
Metaxohori
Agia Galini 13
Mouseio
Kritikis
Ethnologias
Gortys 2
Inia
Ligortinos
Timbaki
Vori
10
Mires
Ormos
Mesaras
Agia
Triada 11
3 Phaistos
6 Agioi Deka
Vagionia
Harakas
12 Matala
Krotos
Tris Ekklisies
Kali Limenes

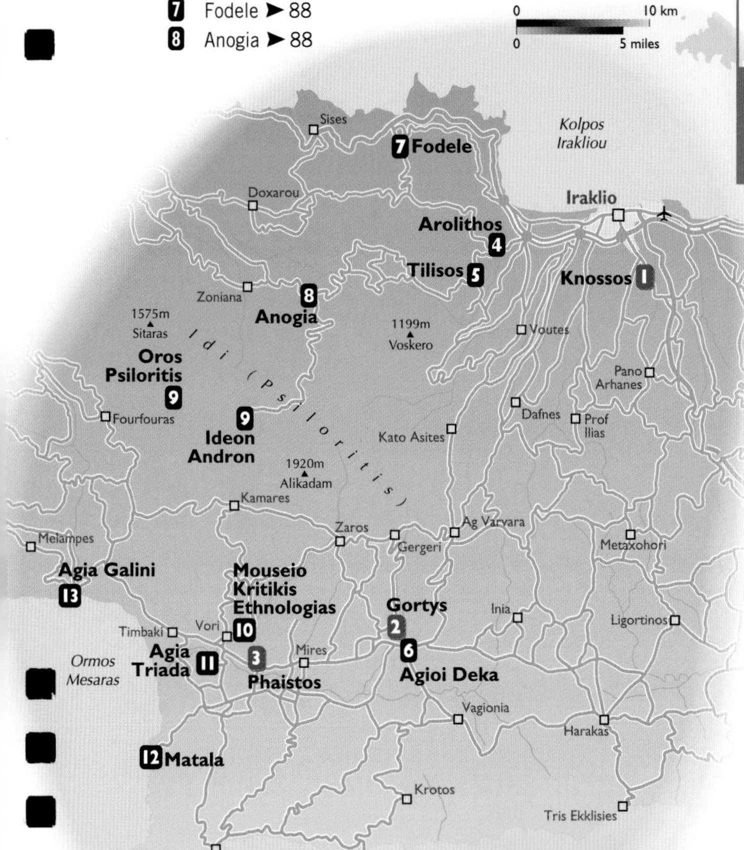

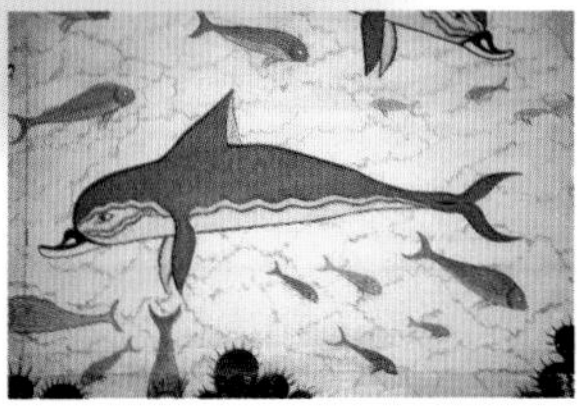

Detail from the dolphin fresco at Knossos

In Three Days

If you're not quite sure where to begin your travels, this itinerary recommends a practical and enjoyable three-day tour of Central Crete, taking in some of the best places to see using the Getting Your Bearings map on the previous page. For more information see the main entries.

Day One

Morning

Try to get to **1 Knossos** (right, ➤ 76–80) by opening time, to have any hope of beating the crowds and heat, and allow a good hour or two at the site. Afterwards, head back towards Iraklio and take the New Road west towards Rethymno, but turn off towards the craft village of **4 Arolithos** (➤ 87). The café at Arolithos is surprisingly good, but don't linger too long.

Afternoon

The ancient site of **5 Tilisos** (➤ 87) closes at 3pm so try to arrive by 2pm to enjoy it before continuing on the winding mountain road to **8 Anogia** (➤ 88–89). If time and daylight allows, drive on to visit the **9 Ideon Andron** (below, ➤ 89), though you should allow at least two hours.

Evening

Spend the night in **Anogia**, where there is a hotel and rooms to rent. A good dining spot is the simple Taverna Skalomata on the right as you leave the village on the road to the cave, which has great views.

Day Two

Morning

Visit the Ideon Andron if you didn't manage it the night before and then head back through Tilisos to reach the New Road. Head west towards Rethymno but look for the turning to **6 Fodele** (➤ 88). Have lunch at one of the simple tavernas here.

Afternoon
Head back towards Iraklio on the New Road but as you reach the city look for the right turn marked to Mires. This is a fast road but makes a pleasant drive as it eventually heads up into the hills. In Agia Varvara watch carefully for the almost hidden little right turn to Zaros.

Evening
After another lovely drive, relax by the pool and later dine at the restaurant of the Idi Hotel (➤ 92) in Zaros.

Day Three

Morning
Explore **Zaros** (➤ 156–157) and go for a short walk up the gorge before heading south on the road to Moires, turning left to reach **2** **Gortys** (right, ➤ 81–83).

Lunch
East of Gortys is the **6** **Church of Agioi Deka** (➤ 87). The village has several authentic tavernas where few tourists venture.

Afternoon
Allow plenty of time for visiting **3** **Phaistos** (below, ➤ 84–86) before deciding where to spend the night: in the small resort of Matala, or the bigger but prettier **13** **Agia Galini** (➤ 91).

Evening
The Lions Restaurant in Matala (➤ 94) has excellent food, while Agia Galini offers numerous choices, including Madame Hortense (➤ 93) and the Onar Restaurant (➤ 94).

❶ Knossos

Historical wonder or archaeologist's fantasy? The Minoan palace of Knossos is Crete's biggest attraction, and its excavation yielded the most important remains of this ancient civilisation. Even if you find its reconstructed rooms and columns a travesty, they are none the less fascinating and help to make sense of the sprawling maze of stone. Unlike many archaeological sites, Knossos provides an intimate glimpse of the lives that might have been lived here.

Covering a vast area of 75 hectares/185 acres (only a portion of which is open to the public), Knossos is the largest of the Minoan palaces. It was built on five levels and had over 1,200 rooms, providing accommodation for a huge court. It is thought that more than 100,000 people lived in and around the palace when the Minoan civilisation was at its height.

Shade is not easy to find at Knossos

Neolithic remains found at Knossos suggest that there were settlers here as far back as 6000 BC. The first Minoan palace was constructed around 2000 BC, but was destroyed in an earthquake three centuries later. What you see today are the remains of the even grander palace that replaced it. Even after this palace was destroyed in the great cataclysm of 1450 BC (▶ 10–13), Knossos remained an important settlement for newcomers to the island well into Roman times. Afterwards it fell into obscurity until a Cretan archaeologist, Minos Kalokairinos – coincidentally named after the ancient priest-kings – discovered the storerooms in 1878.

On the Royal Way at Knossos

A Reconstruction

A few years later, a young Englishman, Arthur Evans (➤ below), became intrigued by the site and bought up the land, and by 1900 a full-scale archaeological dig was under way. In just two years he uncovered most of the palace area, but his hasty methods caused important information to be lost or poorly documented. Of greater controversy was Evans' reconstruction of parts of the palace, which he claimed was necessary to preserve and understand it. There was some truth to this, as the original pillars and beams had been made of wood and as he unearthed room after room, the entire structure was in danger of collapse. Evans incorporated original fragments into new concrete pillars and supports, and restored rooms according to how he believed they would have looked during the Minoan era. Later archaeologists have been highly critical of his romantic re-creations, but Evans' work does give visitors a glimpse of the splendour of the Minoan world, and a means to visualise the frescoed walls, ceremonial staircases and red pillars that supported this multi-storey complex.

Seeing the Palace

With its narrow passageways, connecting rooms, raised walkways and L-shaped steps leading to dead-end landings, Knossos can be confusing. No wonder it has been linked with the mythical labyrinth of King Minos. Rooms are labelled, although they can still be challenging to find even with a map,

Sir Arthur Evans

SIR ARTHUR EVANS

At the entrance to Knossos is a bust of Sir Arthur Evans (1851–1941), excavator of the site. He was a man of many talents, working as a journalist and war correspondent before becoming director of the Ashmolean Museum

in Oxford at the age of 33. Ten years later, in 1894, his job led him to Knossos for the first time and he became intrigued by speculations of an ancient palace buried here. Evans was a wealthy man – and a tenacious one. It took him five years to purchase the land from its Turkish owners. Though his autocratic methods drew much criticism, his findings rewrote the history of the ancient world. He was knighted for his achievements in 1911 and continued to work on the site until 1935, when he was 84 years old.

but you will eventually come across all the interesting areas, sometimes when you least expect it.

Sadly, Knossos has suffered from its own popularity. The sheer number of tourists treading its ancient walls has caused structural problems, and many areas and paths are now roped off. False walkways have been built over the natural stone paths to cater for the tour groups on a beaten trail, but they spoil the character of the site and make it difficult for individual visitors to escape the crowds. The best way to enjoy Knossos is to take your time and use your imagination, or visit off-season.

The entrance is through the **west court**, passing the circular pits where devotional objects were placed at the end of sacred rituals. Turn right, and follow the Corridor of Processions, where you first see the palace frescoes. These show a party of men and women carrying gifts and ceremonial vessels. Evans hired French artists to repaint all of the frescoes on site, once the originals were moved to the Archaeological Museum in Iraklio.

Inside the palace walls, on your left is the **south propylaeum** with its tapering white columns and fresco of a cup-bearer. On your right is a reproduction of the enormous Horns of Consecration, standing where the original fragments were found. Just ahead, in an upper chamber, is the famous fresco of the priest-king.

Evans gave the frescoes and rooms their names, such as the *piano nobile*, taken from the Italian Renaissance. A staircase behind the south propylaeum leads up to it, where there is a view over the central court and the storerooms with their giant storage jars.

Below, in the northwest corner of the court, is the **throne room**, decorated with frescoes of griffins. The gypsum throne is thought to be the oldest in Europe. Opposite is

WATERWORKS

A drainage system of terracotta pipes, ingenious for its time, ran below the palace and incorporated a means to stop or control the flow of water. You can still see parts of this system under grilles and around the edges of the royal chambers.

The colourful griffin frescoes of the Throne Room

The notion of Knossos as the labyrinth of King Minos may be more than just myth. In pre-Hellenic times the word *labrys* meant "double axe" and the ending *nthos* meant "house of" – thus, "house of the double axe". Giant double axes were found at Knossos, and were thought to be a symbol of power.

Detail from the Ladies in Blue fresco

a sunken lustral basin, used for purification. If you can't resist the impulse to pose for a photo, there is a wooden replica for that purpose in the antechamber. The throne room is one of the highlights of the palace and long queues often form as people wait to peer over the threshold.

The heart of Knossos is the **central court**, measuring approximately 55m by 28m (180 feet by 92 feet). Originally surrounded by high walls, it is where the bull-leaping rituals and athletic contests depicted in the frescoes took place.

On the east side of the court, the grand staircase leads down to what Evans believed were the **royal chambers**. This

The royal chambers lay east of the central court

is now also blocked off, but you can descend via a corridor to your left. These are the best-preserved rooms, and though they are built into the slope of a hill, they are lit by a system of large light wells. Look for the king's chamber, whose ante-room is marked with shields and the sign of the double axe. The queen's chamber has a delightful fresco of dolphins. Sadly, the adjacent rooms, which held a clay bathtub and flush toilet, are no longer on view.

To the north of the royal chambers are the **palace workshops** and the magazines of giant storage jaars (*pithoi*), used to store olive oil and wine. A **theatre** with some 500 seats lies northwest of the palace. The royal road, with original paving stones dating from the third millennium BC, leads north and may once have run all the way to the sea.

TAKING A BREAK

As an alternative to the site café try any one of the number of **tavernas** lining the road **outside Knossos**, most of which are touristy and unremarkable but fine for a drink or light meal.

✚ 183 F4
✉ 5km (3 miles) south of Iraklio on Odos Knosou ☎ 2810-231940 🕐 Daily 8–5 (3pm in winter) 🍴 Café (€) 🚌 Bus 2, 4 💶 Expensive ❓ Photography allowed

The Dolphin Fresco adorns the Queen's chamber

KNOSSOS: INSIDE INFO

Top tips Knossos is Crete's most popular attraction and it is always busy, especially in summer. **To avoid the worst of the crowds**, try to be there when the site first opens in the morning, or in the early evening. Midday can also be quieter, when large tour groups leave for lunch. The best time to visit is off-season

■ The **summer heat** is intense and there is little shade; bring water and a hat.

■ Allow two hours to **see the highlights**, more if it is very crowded.

■ If the site's free parking area is full, you'll find **pay-parking areas** on the main road just before Knossos and immediately past the entrance.

2 Gortys

On an island full of Minoan remains, the ruins of this ancient Greco-Roman city give a glimpse of a later era. The core site is small but impressive, with the enormous basilica of Agios Titos and the law code – the first such code to be written down in Europe – inscribed on massive stone blocks. If time allows, you can wander through the surrounding fields and olive groves to discover the scattered remnants of this important city.

Spring flowers adorn the fields around Agios Titos at Gortys

The settlement of Gortys dates back to Minoan times. Built along the River Letheos (also known as the Mitropolitanos) on the fertile Mesara Plain, it prospered and grew under the Dorian Greeks and by the 8th century BC had become the most important city in southern Crete. When the Romans conquered the island in 67 BC, they made Gortys the capital of their province Cyrenaica, which encompassed not only Crete but much of North Africa. A century later, St Titus (► 82) made his base here and set about converting the population – which numbered some 30,000, the largest on Crete – to Christianity. It became the religious as well as the political centre of the island.

Gortys flourished throughout Byzantine times until Saracen raiders sacked the city in AD 824. It never recovered and was soon abandoned. Today its ruins cover a large area, much of which has not yet been excavated.

Agios Titos

The major ruins of Gortys lie within a fenced site on the north side of the road. As you enter, the massive shell of Agios Titos draws you to the left. Built in the 6th century, it is the best-preserved early Christian church on Crete, and was the seat of the archbishops until the Arab invasion. The vaulted central apse gives you an idea of its former magnificence, and there is a small shrine in one of the side aisles. The holy relics of St Titus were kept here until 962, when they were moved to a new church in Iraklio (► 62–63). A service is held here once a year on 23 December, the saint's feast day.

ST TITUS THE APOSTLE

According to tradition, Titus was a descendant of a noble Cretan family. He was well educated and journeyed to Jerusalem, where he became a devoted disciple of St Paul the Apostle and travelled with him on his apostolic missions in Asia and Europe. Paul brought Christianity to the island in around AD 59, and left Titus to establish the Cretan Church. He became Crete's first bishop, and died at the age of 94 in about AD 105.

The Law Code

Beyond the church is an area thought to be the ancient agora, or forum. Here, overlooking the remains of the Roman *odeon* (a small theatre used for musical performances and poetry recitals), is a building sheltering Gortys's greatest find: the law code. Carved by the Dorian Greeks around 500 BC on to massive stone blocks, it represents the earliest known written laws in Europe.

The tablets are arranged in 12 columns standing 3m (10 feet) high. The 600 lines of archaic inscription are read alternately left to right and right to left – a style known as *boustrophedon*, a word which describes the pattern made by an ox plough. They provide invaluable insight into this period of Greek history, particularly its social organisation. The code is actually a series of rulings clarifying laws that pertain to marriage, divorce, adoption, property and rights of inheritance. It also laid down penalties for adultery, rape, assault and other offences. Gortys's population was divided into a hierarchy of rulers, citizens or freemen, serfs and slaves, and the rights and penalties varied greatly among the classes.

Gortys's code of law, in clear detail

The ancient fortress at Gortys, with the Roman *odeon* and the building sheltering the law code

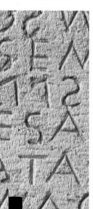

The Acropolis and the Roman City

On the opposite bank of the river you can see the remains of a larger theatre. Above, on the hilltop, are the ancient acropolis and the ruins of a Greek temple, a Roman hall (the *kastro*) and ramparts.

Dotted throughout the open fields on the south side of the main road, stretching back to Agioi Deka, are various remains of the Roman city. Many are little more than scant walls and piles of stone, but it's good fun to seek them out in this atmospheric setting among giant gnarled olive trees. Several of the main sites lie along a track, including the Temple of Isis and Serapis, dedicated to the Egyptian gods. To the south, the Temple of Apollo Pythios with its stepped monumental altar was the main place of worship in pre-Roman times. To the east is the *praetorium*, the Roman governor's palace. Through the fence you can see its paved courtyards, carved columns and capitals and brickwork walls, and the *nymphaeum*, or bath suite.

TAKING A BREAK

On site is an unremarkable but adequate **café**. Otherwise, head back to **Agioi Deka** or press on to **Phaistos**.

🚩 183 E2 ✉ 36km (22 miles) southwest of Iraklio
☎ 28920-31144 🕐 Daily 8–7 (winter 8:30–3) 🍴 Café (€) 🚌 Buses to Phaistos stop at Gortys 💶 Moderate ❓ Photography allowed

---

GORTYS: INSIDE INFO

Top tip It's a steep, hot climb to the top of the acropolis, but you'll get a great overview of the site.

Hidden gem Near the Temple of Apollo Pythios is a small **Roman theatre**, the best preserved on Crete.

Ones to miss The **amphitheatre** and **stadium**, both southeast of the *praetorium*.

3 Phaistos

The Minoan palace at Phaistos is felt by many to be a far more enjoyable site to visit than the better-known Knossos. It stands on a hill overlooking the fertile Mesara Plain, and the fact that it has not been reconstructed allows visitors to view the palace in the best possible way: in the imagination. To see the large central court, the royal apartments, the grand staircase and the nondescript spot where the fabulous Phaistos Disc was found all make for a memorable experience.

The approach to Phaistos is part of its charm, especially if you have already seen Knossos. There are no parking attendants here trying to lure you into their parking lots, just a small car park at the end of a zigzag climb up a little hill. You then walk along the approach to the site to buy a ticket. After entering the site beyond the bookshop, souvenir store and café, you are greeted with a good overall view of the layout.

It is thought that the views were part of Phaistos's original attraction for the Minoans, with the palace built in a way that makes the most of them. Prior to their settlement, it seems others enjoyed the setting, as deposits have been found going back to neolithic and early Minoan periods (3000–2000 BC).

The first palace here, dated from about 1900 BC, is known as the Old Palace and some of its remains can still be seen

Phaistos looks out over the Mesara Plain

The royal apartments surround a small court

on the western edge of the site. Destroyed and repaired twice before its ultimate destruction in an earthquake in 1700 BC, it was replaced by the New Palace, which remained in use until the end of the Minoan civilisation.

Exploring the Palace

The first open space you come to, the **west court**, is a good place to try to picture the palace as it would have been. Go down into the court and look towards the easily recognisable grand staircase. To the right of this are the remains of the western façade of the palace, built to bask in the glow of the setting sun. To the north of the court is the theatre area, and to the south some large storage pits, used principally for grain.

If you climb the grand staircase you'll see to the right the storerooms within the palace itself, where grain and oil were stored in the type of vast storage jars or *pithoi* that can be seen in almost every museum on Crete. It is not known for sure if the commodities stored at the palace were given to the royal

THE PHAISTOS DISC

Only about 15cm (6in) in diameter, the Phaistos Disc, now in the Archaeological Museum in Iraklio (▶ 50–55), is one of the most important and intriguing items ever found on Crete. It dates from between 1700 and 1600 BC and was uncovered in 1903. Baked in clay, the disc has spirals of pictograms on either side, including flowers, people and animals. No one has ever cracked the code, but the most favoured theory is that it was a religious object of some kind, with the symbols perhaps being the words to a prayer or hymn.

family by way of a tithe, or if the building acted as a secure storage area for everyone to use.

To the east of this you enter the impressive central court, a vast open area whose paving dates from 1900 to 1700 BC. If you walk to the southern end of this there are good views over the plain, still a source of grain and oil today. It is the largest and most fertile of all the plains on Crete, producing huge crops of olives, citrus and other fruit, and many types of vegetable.

To the north of the central court the area becomes a little confusing, as the remains are on two levels, but beyond the small south court, which you may be able to identify, are the **royal apartments**. There are many chambers and antechambers here, one set of rooms belonging to the king and another to the queen.

A well provided water for the palace at Phaistos

If you continue walking past these almost to the edge of the site, you can turn right and see on your right the walls and foundations of a row of small buildings. These were the palace archives, where the **Phaistos Disc** (➤ panel, 85) was found, a small object that preserves its secrets, just as the palace of Phaistos preserves its own air of mystery and beauty.

TAKING A BREAK

The **on-site café** is the only place to get something to eat for miles around, but it serves plenty of snacks and simple meals and has a lovely dining terrace with views of the countryside.

➕ 183 D2 ☎ 28920-42315 🕐 Daily 8–7:30 (winter 8:30–3) 🍴 Café
(€) 🚌 From Iraklio take the Phaistos or Matala bus 🚶 Moderate
❓ Photography allowed

At Your Leisure

4 Arolithos

Part of a hotel and purpose-built for tourists, Arolithos may not appeal to everyone. However, if you're yearning to see artisans at work and haven't yet had the chance, this recreation of a traditional village may be what you're looking for. Here you can see weavers, potters and icon painters at work in their ateliers, and learn how *raki* is made in the agricultural history museum

✚ 183 F4 ✉ 10km (6 miles) southwest of Iraklio ☎ 2810-821050 🕐 Apr–Oct Mon–Sat 8–4; Nov–Mar Mon–Fri 9–5, Sat–Sun 10–6, Oct–Mar 🍴 Café (€) 👣 Free ❓ Photography allowed

5 Tilisos

The remains of this ancient Minoan town sit within the village of the same name, a delightful example of the continuity of life through the ages. This small peaceful spot beneath shady pines is little visited and makes a refreshing change from the larger archaeological sites. It centres on three Minoan villas, which are thought to have been part of a larger community. Tilisos was one of the first Minoan sites to be excavated, prompted by the discovery of three giant bronze cauldrons; these and other finds are now in the Archaeological Museum in Iraklio (➤ 50–55). The ruins are well preserved, and you can wander among the stone walls and through doorways into small rooms and courtyards. The olive groves and vineyards, where sweet, dark Malmsey wine has been produced since Venetian times, surround the village.

✚ 183 E4 ✉ 14km (9 miles) southwest of Iraklio ☎ 2810-831241 🕐 Daily 8:30–3 🚌 Iraklio–Anogia bus stops at Tilisos 👣 Inexpensive

6 Agioi Deka

The name of this village translates as the "Holy Ten" and refers to ten early Christian martyrs who were beheaded here in AD 250 by order of the Roman Emperor Decius. They are still highly revered today and two churches in the village are dedicated to them. The Old Church, 14th-century but Byzantine in origin, is a lovely stone building with a tiled roof; it is signposted off the main road, a five-minute walk. Inside are frescoed arches and beautiful woodcarvings, including one of Christ with the martyrs' heads. Two painted icons depict their decapitation, and there is a stone block said to have been used for the execution. The New Church, at the west end of the village towards Gortys, is a simple chapel. Below is a crypt, visible from the outside, where you can peer through an iron gate to see six of the martyr's tombs.

✚ 183 E2 ✉ 35km (22 miles) southwest of Iraklio 🕐 Daily 🚌 From Iraklio take the Phaistos or Matala bus 👣 Free

The bell tower at Agioi Deka

7 Fodele

This pleasant village, surrounded by orange groves, claims to be the birthplace of El Greco (➤ 20–21). A memorial plaque to the painter is on display in the shady town square, and across a small bridge spanning the river is the church, which has many copies of El Greco's works.

To see his alleged birthplace, continue along the path (signposted) out of town beside the orchards for about a kilometre. The house is greatly restored and contains a few displays on the painter's life. Opposite the house is the delightful Church of the PanAgia. Built in the early 14th century, it incorporates the nave of an earlier 8th-century basilica. The baptismal font beside the church – set in the floor for total immersion – also dates from this period. Partially restored frescoes depict angels, saints and scenes from Christ's life.

➕ 183 E4 ✉ 25km (16 miles) west of Iraklio ☎ 2810-521500 (museum) ◎ Museum and church Tue–Sun 9–5 🚌 Direct bus from Iraklio 💰 Inexpensive

8 Anogia

The mountain village of Anogia has suffered greatly at the hands of foreign invaders over the years.

Domenikos Theotokopoulos, better known as El Greco (inset) and his home village, Fodele (above)

The Turks destroyed it twice after rebellions in 1821 and 1866, and in August 1944 German troops shot every male in the village and burned every house to the ground in retaliation for the abduction of General Kreipe (➤ 24). Two statues commemorating the freedom fighters stand in the squares in the upper part of town.

Anogia is best known though for its woven goods and embroidery.

Brightly coloured textiles drape the streets of the lower town and you may see the local women at work inside their shops.

Behind the café tables in Platia Livadhi notice the odd wooden sculpture of Eleftherios Venizelos. It is the work of the late local artist Alkibiades Skoulas, whose son has opened a museum (open daily 9–7) to display his father's works. Anogia is also renowned as a centre of *lyra* music; many top musicians have come from here.

✚ 183 E4
✉ 35km (22 miles) southwest of Iraklio
🚌 Buses from Iraklio and Rethymno

9 Oros Psiloritis and Ideon Andron

At 2,456m (8,060 feet), Mount Ida is the highest summit on Crete. The locals call it Psiloritis, "the high one". Its twin peaks, capped with snow late into spring, are often hidden in cloud, but when the powerful granite bulk is revealed you can understand why it is thought to be Zeus's birthplace (▶ 91).

From Anogia a good paved road winds up through the stark, rocky landscape to the Ideon Andron, 22km (14 miles) away. The trip takes about half an hour each way. Birds of prey circle overhead, and you pass round stone shepherds' huts, or *mitata*. Most are now abandoned but were once used as summer dwellings and for making yoghurt and cheese from sheep's milk. The drive is especially pretty in late spring, when the rugged landscape is ablaze with wild flowers. As you climb higher you may find you are driving through low-lying clouds. Be warned, however, that the road may be closed in winter when it snows.

The road opens out with fine views over the fertile Nida Plateau far below. From here, a 15-minute walk brings you to the Ideon Andron. A place of pilgrimage and cult worship since Minoan times, it yielded a wealth of artefacts from throughout Greece and is mentioned in the works of Greek philosophers Plato and Pythagoras. Steps lead down into the cave but you may find its history is the most exciting part – it is relatively shallow and has no impressive natural features.

✚ 183 D3 (Ideon Andron), 182 A3 (Oros Psiloritis) ✉ 50km (31 miles) southwest of Iraklio 🕐 Always open, except in winter when the road is closed if there is snow 🚌 No public transport 🆓 Free

The twin peaks of Mount Ida

10 Mouseio Kritikis Ethnologias

Located off the beaten track in the village of Voroi, near Phaistos, this excellent folk museum, founded by a local man, is one of the best of its kind on the island. The items are attractively laid out, with information

Displays at the Ethnology Museum in Voroi

panels in English. Among the ground-floor exhibits are agricultural and domestic items, such as terracotta beehives used since Pharaonic times, furniture, pottery and architecture. Another beautiful collection consists of woven blankets and textiles, and there is an interesting study of door patterns and their relation to status.

The highlight upstairs is a fascinating display of 25 types of baskets, made with different techniques and for different purposes. You can also see musical instruments and wonderful photos of people and festivals.

➕ 183 D2 ✉ 3km (2 miles) north of Phaistos at Voroi (park on the main street and follow signs to the museum) ☎ 28920-91112
🕐 Apr–Oct daily 8:30–3 💰 Moderate
❓ Photography allowed

11 Agia Triada

This Minoan site is small-scale after nearby Phaistos, but its intimate nature is the very reason it should be visited. The main ruins consist of a small palace or large royal villa, built in about 1600 BC and destroyed, like many other Minoan sites, by a huge fire around 1450 BC. Staircases show that the palace had several levels. Fabulous mosaics, jewellery, pottery and other finds have been made here, all now on display at the Archaeological Museum in Iraklio (➤ 50–55). There is also a cemetery, and the remains of the small town that built up around the palace: a market, shops, houses and workshops. Part of Agia Triada's delight is that no one is quite sure what it was or who lived here, as there are no references to it in existing Minoan records.

➕ 183 D2 ✉ 3km (2 miles) northwest of Phaistos ☎ 28920-91360 🕐 Tue–Sun 10–3 🚌 Bus to Phaistos 💰 Inexpensive
❓ Photography allowed

The harvester vase found at Agia Triada

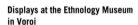

⓬ Matala

Matala's days as a hippie haven are long gone, but its caves continue to draw visitors. The caves are man-made, cut into the sandstone cliffs by Romans and early Christians and used as catacombs. Local people inhabited them until the 1960s, when foreign hippie troglodytes moved in. The caves are now fenced off to discourage overnight stays. Some have carved doorways, windows and benches.

The caves form a backdrop to Matala's beach, wide and curving round the bay with taverna balconies overlooking the beach. Otherwise, it's a slightly tacky town with touristy restaurants and shops, tending to attract a young, boisterous crowd. It should be noted that outside of the April–October tourist season, everything in Matala is shut and the town is deserted.

➕ 183 D2 ✉ 59km (35 miles) southwest of Iraklio ◉ Caves open Apr–Sep daily 10–4 🚌 Several buses daily from Iraklio 💷 Inexpensive

⓭ Agia Galini

Agia Galini is a pretty resort on the southern coast. Nestled into the surrounding mountains, its whitewashed buildings, dripping with bright bougainvillaea and jasmine, rise up the steep streets from a picturesque harbour. It's now pretty much given over to tourism, and the traffic-free streets in the centre of this former fishing village are lined with shops and restaurants. The long strip of beach has more

Agia Galini rises up from the harbour

rocks than sand, but is pleasantly fringed with tavernas. Though the town can get busy, it is a real delight out of season.

➕ 182 C2 ✉ 45km (28 miles) southeast of Rethymno 🚌 Buses from Rethymno

BIRTHPLACE OF ZEUS

Mythologists argue over whether the god Zeus was born in the Ideon Cave or the Diktaean Cave (▶ 114). His mother, Rhea, had to bear the child in secrecy because his father, Kronos, Lord of the Titans, had devoured his other offspring, fearing they would someday dethrone him. Guardian warriors, the Kouretes, hid baby Zeus's cries with the clashing of their shields. When Kronos finally tracked Rhea down, she fooled him by giving him a stone wrapped in swaddling clothes to swallow. Zeus grew up with the shepherds on Mount Ida, protected by his grandmother Gaia.

Where to... Stay

Prices
Prices are for a double room per night in high season including taxes
€ under €70   €€ €70–€150   €€€ over €150

AGIA GALINI

El Greco Hotel €

Ideally placed halfway between the town centre and the town beach (on the left of the main road as you first enter Agia Galini), this is a decent and inexpensive hotel with its own car park opposite. The blue and white frontage matches the bright rooms, those at the back being slightly more expensive because of their balconies and sea views. The buffet breakfast varies each day and can be taken on the terrace at the back.

🚹 182 C2 ☒ Agia Galini ☎ 28320-91187
🕒 Apr–Oct

Fevro Hotel €

This 50-room hotel can be found on the right after the road into Agia Galini descends almost to sea level. Look for where there is a sharp turn left towards the harbour – that's if you can see the hotel name, as the entire building is almost obscured by the most wonderful cascade of colourful bougainvillaea. The clean and simple rooms are a reasonable size, with plain white walls and dark wood furniture. Some have views of the town, and those lower down have "no views but not so many stairs"!

🚹 182 C2 ☒ Agia Galini ☎ 08320-91275

MATALA

Armonia Hotel €

This delightful small hotel is a real find. As you approach Matala on the main road look for it on the left, a white building (covered in bougainvillaea) with a pool. It is well outside the town so you will need a car, but it makes a great getaway for nature lovers and walkers. Most of the 27 rooms are in small blocks behind the hotel.

🚹 183 D2 ☒ Matala ☎ 28920-4573;
www.armonia-matala.com 🕒 May–Oct

Hotel Zafiria €

The main hotel in Matala is the 70-room Zafiria, easily found on your left as the main road enters the town centre. The rooms are typically mid-range – simple and clean – but all have a shower, a radio and a balcony. Some look out towards the sea, others to the hills behind. The hotel has its own bar and restaurant, and owns the mini-market across the street. Although nothing fancy,

this makes a good, reasonably priced base.

🚹 183 D2 ☒ Matala ☎ 28920-45112/45747/45386;
www.zafiria-matala.com 🕒 Apr–Oct

ZAROS

Idi Hotel €

Situated on the edge of the mountain town of Zaros and popular with walkers, the Idi Hotel is an unexpected treat. With its swimming pool and tennis court, bar and Votomos Taverna (▶ 94), it represents excellent value for money. Rooms are in the main hotel block or separate buildings in the beautiful gardens, and are pine-panelled with telephones and air-conditioning. The staff can advise on walking in the Zaros Gorge (▶ 156–157) and other areas. Activities here include olive-picking, harvesting honey and visits to *raki* distilleries

🚹 183 E2 ☒ Zaros ☎ 28940-31302;
www.idi-hotel.com 🕒 All year

Where to...
Eat and Drink

Prices
Prices are for a two-course meal for one person, excluding drinks and tips
€ under €20   €€ €20–€40   €€€ over €40

AGIA GALINI

Charlie's Place €€

Charlie's Place is a popular spot with great character. Wooden tables are crammed together in one room, spilling into the street. The kitchen is at the back, a tiny place where the owner, Charlie, a Greek-Cypriot, cooks, grills meat, prepares drinks and writes out bills in a whirr of frenetic activity. The menu is small and traditionally Greek, and the meat comes from local farms. One of the busiest places in town, so arrive early or be prepared to wait.

✚ 182 C2 ☒ Agia Galini ☎ 28320-91065
🕑 Daily 7pm–late

Madame Hortense €€

Climb the flight of wooden stairs and pass a large collection of evocative black and white photos of Cretan characters and scenes to reach a large room with wooden flooring and great open views over the harbour. There are plenty of Greek and Cretan specialities on the menu, which has an extract from *Zorba the Greek* on the front explaining the restaurant's name. Chicken with peas and olives is one

speciality, as is the house version of *kleftiko*: lamb wrapped in filo pastry and baked in the oven. The service includes an aperitif of ouzo served in a beautiful little bottle of coloured glass and a small plate of *mezedes*. The restaurant has become a popular venue for wedding receptions for British couples

✚ 182 C2 ☒ Agia Galini ☎ 28320-91215
🕑 Daily 6pm–late

"O Faros" €

This unpretentious little fish taverna, one of the oldest in town, is run by a fishing family serving whatever they catch that day. The tables on the pedestrian street are waited on by the friendly father or his cheerful son, who will invite you into the kitchen to choose your fish. They also offer daily cruises to local beaches and islands, including the chance to catch your own fish and have it cooked for you the same evening.

✚ 182 C2 ☒ Agia Galini ☎ 28320-91346;
fax: 28320-91346 🕑 Daily 6:30pm–late

Onar €€

This large, two-storey restaurant has an upstairs roof garden and a lower floor, both of which have good views out over the bustling harbour. Inside is modern and spacious with brick half-walls and lots of timber, plus attractive murals and wall hangings. Excellent food and wonderfully friendly service are the hallmarks here, with food grilled over charcoal a speciality. One excellent dish is barracuda fillet with a tomato and garlic sauce.

✚ 182 C2 ☒ Agia Galini ☎ 28320-91121
🕑 Mar–Nov daily 8am–1am

Potamida €€

Standing right by the beach, the Potamida is one of the biggest restaurants in a row of cafés and tavernas, distinctive with its bright blue and white décor. It is open all day and has sunbeds and umbrellas on the beach. The menu offers a huge choice of dishes, particularly salads and pastas, but fresh seafood is the speciality.

Indeed, you might see the chef wading into the sea in the morning with his harpoon gun to catch the fish of the day.

➕ 182 C2 ⊠ Agia Galini ☎ 28320-91121
🕐 Mar–Oct daily 9am–11:30pm

MATALA

Corali €€

The lemon paintwork of the Corali stands out on Matala's little square. Here food is served from breakfast time until the last customers leave. You'll have to wait till lunchtime if you want hot dishes though; these include a good range of the usual Greek fare and fresh fish, but there are pizzas too if you fancy a change.

➕ 183 D2 ⊠ Matala ☎ 28920-45744
🕐 Apr–Oct daily 10am–late

Lions Restaurant €€

Looking right over the beach, Lions has an upper taverna/bar where you can have coffee, drinks and snacks, or choose from the full menu in the slightly smarter restaurant

downstairs. The chef lived in Australia for 30 years and as a result the menu here is more eclectic than in many Crete restaurants: it's one of the few places on Crete where you'll see Coquilles St Jacques, for example, while another speciality is sole stuffed with crabmeat.

➕ 183 D2 ⊠ Matala ☎ 28920-45108
🕐 Apr–Oct daily 9am–late

Skala €

To find Skala, go to the very far end of the waterfront to the south and walk through what seems like the last taverna and up some steps; the restaurant is perched on top of the rocks beyond. Family owned, it's a very simple but very popular place, with a great view across the water to the beach. The large open dining terrace with cheerful blue and white walls and doors fills quickly, so arrive early. Fish is the speciality on the menu, and depending on the season might include red mullet, red snapper, perch, lobster, octopus and mussels.

➕ 183 D2 ⊠ Matala ☎ 28920-45489
🕐 Apr–Oct daily 9am–late

La Strada €€

The cheery blue and white tables on the street contrast with the rustic Italian decor inside, where there is more seating, as well as on the roof terrace. Outside a blackboard lists the day's specials, while the menu has a whole page devoted to pizzas and other Italian dishes, although the wine list is resolutely Greek. La Strada is always busy but the service is brisk and efficient.

➕ 183 C2 ⊠ Agia Galini ☎ 28320-91053
🕐 Daily noon–3, 6–midnight

Taverna Giannis €

This is a real family taverna, found on the right just beyond the small main square. It's as simple as you could get, with a few tables inside and out, serving barrel wine only. You could try one of their specials, such as a Cretan plate of octopus, squid, potatoes and vegetables, or opt for one of the simple Greek

dishes, including grilled fresh fish. While the choices may be unsurprising they are very well prepared, the standard of cooking is excellent and service friendly.

➕ 183 D2 ⊠ Matala ☎ Apr–Oct daily noon–late

ZAROS

Votomos Taverna €€

This rural restaurant, situated next to the Idi Hotel (▶ 92) by a stream and small watermill, specialises in trout from the nearby hatchery. Options include plain trout, salmon trout and smoked trout, along with a range of other fish and meat dishes, with wine from the barrel or from the short list of Cretan wines. There's both indoor and outdoor seating, as well as a large stage used for occasional live music. In the summer months it's advisable to book to avoid waiting for a table.

➕ 183 E3 ⊠ Zaros ☎ 28940-31302
🕐 Mar–Oct daily 11am–midnight;
Nov–Feb Sat–Sun 11am–midnight

Where to... Shop

VILLAGE CRAFTS

You'll find the usual tourist shops and stalls at the entrance to **Fodele**, but for something special try **Atelier Keramos**, the ceramic studio of Manolis Grammatikakis and Paraskevi Laskari-Grammatikaki (tel: 2810-521362), whose family has been making pottery for four generations. They incorporate new designs into traditional styles to create both useful and decorative pieces. Many designs are available, or you can design your own piece. **Anogia** is one of the best-known villages on Crete for textiles, but don't overlook the handicrafts in smaller villages. At **Tilisos**, for example, right next to the archaeological site, a woman and her daughters have a tiny shop where they sell beautiful and intricate handmade embroidered pieces at very good prices.

Colourful blankets, wall hangings, bags and other pieces made on the loom, or handstitched embroidery or lacework, such as tablecloths or curtains, are items to look for, but be aware that more and more textiles are imported these days. One way to tell if an article is handmade is to look on the back. If the stitching there is rough and uneven, it's probably hand-done, whereas smooth stitches indicate a factory-sewn item. Another tip is to look for shops where the proprietor herself is working on a piece of embroidery or on a loom. You are welcome to watch, but be prepared for a sales pitch afterwards.

At **Arolithos**, where there is a small row of workshops, you can watch potters, weavers, jewellery-makers, silversmiths, icon painters and other artists create beautiful pieces using time-honoured methods and designs.

AGIA GALINI

Among the many shops in Agia Galini a few stand out. **Labyrinth** (tel: 28320-91057), in the tiny pedestrianised centre, is where Savas Tsimpouras makes beautiful gold and silver jewellery, as well as rings and necklaces adorned with rose quartz, tourmaline and other precious stones. He also makes replicas of the honeybee brooch in Iraklio's Archaeological Museum (▶ 50–55) and other Minoan works, and will create pieces to order. A few doors away, next to the Blue Bar, is Eli, an artist who creates outstanding pottery in her workshop at the back of the shop. Her work, from female figures to mobiles to beautifully shaped vases, many etched with dolphins or sun motifs, is unique.

You will also find lots of olive-wood souvenirs in Agia Galini. Try **Wood Shop Maria** in the centre for a good selection of handmade items. **Le Shop**, just round the corner from La Strada restaurant (▶ 94), sells a nice range of quality leather items, silver jewellery and books and newspapers in several languages, including novels and books about Crete.

MATALA

Matala has a covered market area lined with souvenir stalls, but nothing outstanding is to be found here. The nicest shop is **Natura Minoika**, on the main street, which sells natural Cretan products such as herbed olive oils, soaps and sponges, and popular art made from olive wood. Here you can buy mortar and pestle sets, unusual coffee and sugar measures, candle holders, wine holders, honeypots and beautiful wooden bowls of various sizes.

Where to...
Be Entertained

NIGHTLIFE

Agia Galini is the hotspot for nightlife in central Crete. Young Cretans from the Mesara area meet at the **Alibi Bar** by the waterfront to stop for a drink and exchange information. **Paradiso (Paradise Bar)**, a roof-garden bar up the steps from the waterfront, is a favourite for dancing and has a happy hour from 10pm to midnight.

Also good for dancing are **Cactus**, **Juke Box** and **Escape**, all near each other by the harbour. Here the music hots up after 11 pm. Smaller, atmospheric spots for socialising over good music include **Blue Bar**, opposite Faros taverna, and **Jazz n'Jazz** at the top end of the central pedestrianised area.

In **Matala**, on the road heading south parallel to the beach, the place to be is the famous **Rock Bar**, and it is not unusual to find young people from Iraklio who have come for the evening. Despite the name, a range of music is played. **Marinero** next door is another option. For a Latin beat and world music over cocktails, try **Kantari** on the main square.

Club opening hours vary widely, with some (particularly those that are also cafés) being open all day, others opening early evening and some not till 10pm or so. Clubs and discos seldom open before 10 or 11pm and don't really get going till midnight. During high season in summer, clubs and discos are open nightly, but in low season they are often open only on weekends.

GREEK MUSIC

If it's Greek music you're after, there are "Greek nights" including live music and dancing at many tavernas on weekends in summer. Travel agencies in **Agia Galini** can also book Greek nights for you.

INTERNET CAFÉS

A good internet café is the **Alexander Bar**, at the east end of the waterfront in Agia Galini. **Café Bar Christos** in the pedestrianised centre has internet access as well as pool tables and a games arcade.

SPORTS

A host of **watersports** is available at Agia Galini, including waterskiing, paragliding, jet skis, banana boats and paddleboats. Enquire at the **Watersports Café** at the start of the beach.

Tour operators in town can book **boat trips** to more remote beaches, such as Agios Georgios and Agios Pavlos, and to the sandy beaches of Paximadia Island, 12km (7 miles) offshore. There are also trips to the Samaria and Impros gorges (▶ 140–141 and 145), or Preveli Beach and Monastery (▶ 144). The **Argonaut**, operated by the owners of the "O Faros" (▶ 93), will take you on cruises, fishing trips or excursions to Gavdos Island and local beaches.

For boat trips from Matala to nearby Red Beach and elsewhere, check with a local travel agent. Some of Matala's beaches are spawning grounds for sea turtles, an endangered species.

The **Melanouri Horse Farm** (tel: 28920-45040) is signposted from the village of Pitsidia, northeast of Matala. Here the riding centre caters for all ages, including children, and offers rides along Kommos Beach and full-moon rides – a chance to explore the beautiful and fertile Mesara Plain.

Eastern Crete

Getting Your Bearings

Northeastern Crete has seen some of the densest tourism development on the island, particularly in the north between Iraklio and Kolpos Mirampellou (Gulf of Mirabello), where bustling resorts have gobbled up the coastal landscape. Beyond the bay, however, the far eastern region holds some of the most stunning scenery on the island, from rugged mountains to an unexpected palm beach.

Crete's main centre of package tourism lies east of the capital, stretching along the north coast to Malia. Here a string of burgeoning resorts have all but usurped the old villages with cheek-by-jowl hotels, apartments, restaurants, bars, travel agencies and souvenir shops. Agios Nikolaos, set prettily around a little lake, is another bustling centre. Amid this hedonistic coastal strip, the ancient palace of Malia and the Minoan town of Gournia anchor this changing landscape to the past.

A short drive inland takes you into another world. The provincial town of Neapoli is a gateway to the windmills and timeless farming villages of the Lasithiou Plateau. High in the Dikti Mountains is the birthplace of the Greek god Zeus. At Kritsa, the fresco-covered Church of Panagia Kera is an artistic jewel.

A stunning coastal drive, not to be missed, brings you further east to Sitia, with its attractive waterfront and relaxed pace. From here you can strike out across a starkly beautiful mountainous landscape to reach Moni Toplou, the palm-fringed Paralia Vai and the Minoan palace at Zakros.

Ierapetra, Europe's southernmost town, is the largest on the south coast, with more fine beaches at small resorts to either side.

Kato Gouves
Limenas Chersonisou
Chani Kokkini
Stalida
Malia Palati
Malia
Mohos
Episkopi
Kastelli
Tzermiado
Dikteon Andron
Thrapsano
Arkalohori
D i k
2141m Afendis Hristos
Kato Kastelliana
Ano Viannos
Keratokambos

The village of
Kritsa

| 0 | | 20 km |
| 0 | | 10 miles |

Skinias

Neapoli 719m Loutsi

10 Spinalonga

9 Elounda

Paralia Vai

14 O Grandes

8

1564m Katharo Tsivi

Kritsa 2 2

3 Agios Nikolaos

Panagia Kera

1485m Platia Korifi

4

Gournia

Moni Toplou 13

5 Sitia

Skopi

Palekastro

Kolpos Mirambellou

Sfaka

1237m Askordalia

803m Prinias

Sitanos

Vori

Ziros

15 Zakros Palati

Anatoli

Kato Horio

Koutsouras

Atherinolakkos

12

Mirtos

11 Ierapetra

Page 97: A
church in
Ierapetra

Left: Boats at
Elounda

In Five Days

If you're not quite sure where to begin your travels, this itinerary recommends a practical and enjoyable five-day tour of Eastern Crete, taking in some of the best places to see using the Getting Your Bearings map on the previous page. For more information see the main entries.

Day One

Morning/Lunch
Get an early start from **1 Malia** (right, sacrificial altar, ➤ 102–103) or **8 Neapoli** (➤ 114). Follow the drive around the **Lasithiou Plateau** (➤ 160–162) and visit the **7 Dikteon Andron** (➤ 114–115). The Kali Mera taverna just west of Psichro is the closest place to the cave to eat, or drive on to the Platanos taverna, set around Krasi's giant plane tree.

Afternoon
Aim to reach Malia Palace by 2pm to explore the ancient ruins, then hit the beach for a swim.

Evening
You could stay overnight in Malia and have dinner at one of the tavernas in the old village, alternatively return to Neapoli for the night and have a pizza at Il Palazzo (➤ 122).

Day Two

Morning/Lunch
Visit **2 Kritsa** (left, typical blue pottery) and **Panagia Kera** (➤ 104–105) early to beat the crowds. Have lunch by the beach at the Barko restaurant (➤ 121) in Agios Nikolaos.

Afternoon
Drive to **9 Elounda** (➤ 115) and take the boat trip to **10 Spinalonga Island** (➤ 115).

Evening
Stay in Elounda and dine by the waterfront at the Ferryman Taverna (➤ 121) or Vritomartes (➤ 122), or head for Agios Nikolaos.

Day Three

Morning/Lunch
Drive to **3** Agios Nikolaos (left, Kitro Platia Beach), and visit the Archaeological Museum (➤ 106–107) and other sights, then have lunch in the pretty courtyard of the Pelagos restaurant (➤ 121).

Afternoon/Evening
Explore the Minoan ruins at **4** Gournia(➤ 108–109) then make the short drive south across the isthmus to **Ierapetra** (➤ 116). From here, continue west to **12** Mirtos (➤ 116) for a relaxing drink beside the sea. Stay the night here and have dinner at Taverna Akti (➤ 122).

Day Four

Morning
Return via Ierapetra to the north coast and take the spectacular cliff road to **5** Sitia (right, ➤ 110–112).

Lunch/Afternoon
Have lunch at one of Sitia's waterfront tavernas, but tear yourself away by 2pm to visit the town's Archaeological Museum (➤ 111). Afterwards, sun yourself on the town beach.

Evening
Visit the Folklore Museum (➤ 111) and return to the waterfront for dinner at O Mixos (➤ 122).

Day Five

Morning/Lunch
Get an early start from Sitia for the winding drive to **15** Zakros Palati (➤ 118). Relax over an early lunch at Kato Zakros Bay Restaurant (➤ 122).

Afternoon
On the return through Palaiokastro continue north for a swim at **14** Paralia Vai (➤ 117). Leave by 4:30pm to reach **13** Moni Toplou (➤ 117), which is open until 6pm.

Evening
Return to Sitia for dinner at The Cretan House (➤ 122).

❶ Malia Palati

Set on a flat plain along the northern coast, the island's third largest Minoan palace may lack the grandeur of Phaistos or Knossos, but the beautiful reddish hues of its substantial stone walls give it an evocative beauty of its own. It is also less crowded and easier to fathom than its bigger sisters, making for an enjoyable place to wander back in time.

First built around 1900 BC, Malia Palace was destroyed by earthquakes and rebuilt around 1650 BC, after which it stood for another 200 years. The ruins date from the latter period. After its discovery in 1915 excavations were taken over by the French Archaeological School in Athens. These are still continuing, and the remains of a substantial town are being unearthed to the north and west of the main site. Some areas that were built of mud brick have been placed under canopies to prevent them being eroded by rain and wind.

Giant *pithoi* (storage jar) standing in the grounds at Malia

Exploring the Ruins

The entrance to the palace is through the west court. You can weave your way through the thick stone walls of the west magazines (storerooms). Alternatively, turn right and head to the southwest corner where there are eight round granary pits. Follow the south side to a wide stone-paved passage that leads into the central court, a huge space measuring 48m by 22m (157 feet by 72 feet).

The **west wing** held the most important sections of the palace, including the loggia, an elevated room looking on to the court, reached by the grand staircase alongside. Below this a hall leads into the pillar crypt, a place of religious ritual. In the court's southwest corner is another large staircase, and beside this is Malia's famous *kernos*. This circular slab of limestone with 34 depressions set around a central hollow is thought to have been a kind of altar in which seed or grain offerings were placed. It may also have been a gaming board.

One of Malia's more curious features is the large number of storage areas throughout the palace. The entire east wing was given over to more magazines used for storing liquids in

Protection for the precious remains of Malia Palace

giant *pithoi* (storage jars) placed in sunken pits, complete with drainage channels for spillage.

On the north side is the hypostyle, or pillared hall, and north court. To the west of this were the royal apartments. Two magnificent giant *pithoi* stand guard along the palace's northern edge. Malia yielded some outstanding artefacts, now in the Archaeologial Museum in Iraklio (➤ 50–55). The famous honeybee pendant was discovered at the grave complex called Chryssolakos (pit of gold), to the northeast of the palace.

TAKING A BREAK

You can buy **drinks and snacks** from a van in the car park, but you'll have to return to **Malia town** for more substantial refreshment.

✚ 184 C4 ☎ 28970-31597 🕓 Tue–Sun 8:30–3 🚌 Buses to/from Malia town stop at the palace 💷 Moderate ❓ Photography allowed

---

MALIA PALATI: INSIDE INFO

Top tip For the best **photographs**, visit in the late afternoon when the light brings out the warm colours of the red stone.

Getting there The palace is **3km (2 miles) beyond Malia village**, signposted off the New Road.

One to miss The museum is **very small** with only a site model and some photos and diagrams on the wall.

❷ Kritsa & Panagia Kera

The tiny Byzantine Church of Panagia Kera is one of the most famous on Crete, renowned for the 14th- and 15th-century frescoes that cover almost every inch of its interior walls with vivid religious scenes. It stands just outside the traditional village of Kritsa, as does the archaeological site of Lato, and a visit combining all three makes for a fascinating and contrasting couple of hours.

Kritsa

Said to be the largest village on Crete, Kritsa sits in the low hills about 10km (6 miles) inland from the busy resort of Agios Nikolaos. It can be very crowded when coach parties descend and hundreds of people wander the steep streets searching for the best of the local handicrafts. Weavings, embroidery, lace and leatherware are all here in abundance, and with better prices than you will pay in shops in the resort towns on the coast. When the visitors depart, Kritsa reverts to being an ordinary Cretan village, and an attractive one, too, with its backdrop of mountains and views in places down to the coast.

Above: Just one of many frescoes in the Panagia Kera

Lato

Signposted from Kritsa, 3km (2 miles) north, is the site of ancient Lato. It is well worth visiting both for the drive along the zigzagging valley road up to the site and the magnificent views over the valley when you get there. Lato is one of Crete's lesser-known sites, with comparably fewer visitors, and is all the better for that.

It dates from the Dorian period, which followed the Minoan and Mycenaean eras, when the Dorian people, originally from northern Greece, ruled Crete and much of the mainland from about 1100 BC until the arrival of the Romans in 69 BC. Lato was an important city, as can be seen by the extent of the remains along the hillside. Excavations did not begin until 1957 and much work still needs to be done. Areas uncovered so far include the agora, or market-place, steps that were part of a theatre, the foundations of shops and artisans' workshops and what was probably the original gate to the old city. The best part of the experience is simply being there, however, as the site has a unique charm.

Panagia Kera

The highlight of eastern Crete is the delightful Church of Panagia Kera, a little domed beige building with just three tiny aisles. It is reached by a path from the main road. With the exception of the stone floors, the church interior is covered in frescoes. Some of the colours are a little dulled with time, but the details are as clear and as beautiful as when they were first painted during the 14th and 15th centuries. The sheer volume of images, including icons of the saints, biblical scenes and graphic depictions of the punishments that sinners can expect in Hell, is overwhelming.

Below: Walking through history at Lato

TAKING A BREAK

There are several cafés and tavernas in **Kritsa**. The **Paradise Snack Bar** opposite Panagia Kera is open all day for everything from coffee to meals.

Lato
185 D3 · Kritsa · Tue–Sun 8:30–3 (but see below) · Free · Photography allowed

Panagia Kera
185 D3 · Kritsa · Daily 8:30–3, but is sometimes shut without access to a key · Buses to Kritsa from Agios Nikolaos · Moderate · No photography allowed

KRITSA & PANAGIA KERA: INSIDE INFO

Top tips Early morning and late afternoon are the quietest times to visit Kritsa.

Hidden gem In the central aisle of Panagia Kera, on the right-hand side near the door, is a delightful and moving portrait of the *Virgin and Child*; the two figures are exchanging the most loving of looks.

Getting there The Church of Panagia Kera is on the right as you approach Kritsa from Agios Nikolaos, but the signs are small. Easier to spot is the Paradise Snack Bar, on the left-hand side of the road. The ticket office is opposite.

❸ Agios Nikolaos

The town of Agios Nikolaos with its twin harbours is one of the most attractive on Crete. Its popularity means that it is also one of the busiest, but if you don't mind the crowds you can enjoy its restaurants and nightlife. It also has an excellent archaeological museum with fine Minoan treasures.

Life centres round the two harbours, although the inner one is actually a tiny lake, linked to the main harbour by a narrow channel. Lake Voulismeni is also known as the Bottomless Lake, a slight exaggeration but it does have very steep sides and a middle depth of some 64m (210 feet). Bars, cafés, restaurants and souvenir shops line the lake and harbour, and the area buzzes from morning till night.

The town has always been a port, in ancient times for the inland city of Lato (➤ 104–105), and later for the Venetians. They named the town after a 10th-century church dedicated to St Nicholas, and they also dubbed the gulf on which it stands Mirabello, or Beautiful View.

Along the waterfront north of the harbour is a small **aquarium**. Although housed in just one room, it is well laid out with lots of displays and information panels, mostly in English. The many tanks contain a host of creatures, from endearing little red-eared turtles and starfish, to octopuses and eels and other inhabitants of the local waters.

The cathedral of Agia Triada

Archaeological Museum

It's a steep climb, but one worth making, up to the town's excellent Archaeological Museum. Take the rooms, arranged around a small interior courtyard, in a clockwise direction.

After various displays of unusual objects, such as the earliest known fish-hooks on Crete and the longest early-Minoan dagger, you come to the museum's star attraction: the **Goddess of Mirtos**. This exquisite piece, dating from around 2500 BC, depicts an unusual bell-shaped figure holding a jug in her stick-like arms. It was probably used for a fertility ritual. Further on are ceramics, coins, votive figures and many unique objects, such as a late Minoan burial *pithos* from Krya with the skeleton

Lakeside dining in Agios Nikolaos

inside. In Room IX, a local Roman 1st century tomb was found to contain the skull of an athlete crowned with a golden laurel and a silver coin resting in his jaw – to pay the ferryman to the Underworld.

TAKING A BREAK

Several places to eat fringe the **harbour and the lake**, but one of the established favourites for visitors and locals is **Barko** (➤ 121), open from breakfast till late.

✚ 185 D3

Archaeological Museum
✉ Palaiologou 68 ☎ 28410-24943 🕐 Tue–Sun 8:30–3 🚌 Parking in streets and car park near by 💷 Inexpensive ❓ No flash photography

Aquarium
✉ Akti Koundourou 30 ☎ 28410-28030 🕐 Daily 10–9, Mar–Oct 🚌 Parking opposite along the waterfront 💷 Expensive ❓ No photography

Folklore Museum
✉ Palaiologou 2 ☎ 28410-25093 🕐 Sun–Fri 9:30–1:30, 7–9 🚌 Parking further on around the waterfront 💷 Inexpensive ❓ Photography allowed

---

AGIOS NIKOLAOS: INSIDE INFO

Top tip Traffic is bad, so **avoid driving into the centre** if you can. One option is to park in the streets on the hill where the Archaeological Museum stands.

Hidden gem The 12th-century **Church of Panagia Vrefotrofou**, near the town beach at the western end of the marina, is said to be the oldest church on Crete. Some of the frescoes are thought to date back to the 8th and 9th centuries, with the building itself going back to the 7th century. If it is closed, ask at the nearby Minos Palace Hotel for the key.

Must see The **Goddess of Mirtos** in the Archaeological Museum.

One to miss The **Folklore Museum** by the channel between the lakes is not bad, but could be skipped if time is short.

4 Gournia

Crete's great Minoan palaces tend to get all the glory, overshadowing the other surviving remnants from the civilisation, which was widespread, particularly in the east. Gournia is the largest town yet uncovered and its superbly preserved ruins give a fascinating insight into everyday life in Minoan times. This was a real work-a-day town, where tradesmen such as potters, bronzesmiths and carpenters went about their daily affairs.

Though Gournia was settled in early Minoan times, the ruins you see today date from around 1500 BC, when the town was at its peak. It flourished because of its splendid position above Kolpos Mirampellou (Gulf of Mirabello), making it commercially as well as strategically important. It had its own harbour and traded with Ierapetra on the south coast via an overland route across the isthmus (at 12km/7 miles the narrowest point on the island), thus avoiding the dangerous sea journey round the eastern shores.

Destroyed in the cataclysm of 1450 BC (➤ 11, panel), Gournia rose from its ashes during Mycenaean times but was finally abandoned in 1200 BC. A young American archaeologist, Harriet Boyd Hawes (1871–1945), excavated it around the same time that Phaistos and Knossos were being excavated (1901).

Exploring Gournia

On entering the site, you immediately notice how well preserved it is. The foundations of hundreds of houses, up to a metre or more high, spread up the hillside; these were the basements, used as storerooms or workshops, with living areas in the upper storeys that have long since vanished. Tools found in some of these buildings identified various tradesmen and craftsmen, farmers and fishermen, providing great insight into domestic life in Minoan times. Cobbled streets, wide enough for pack animals but not wheeled carts, wound through the town, dividing it into seven neighbourhoods. Even today, mountain villages on Crete follow this layout.

You can take the path straight ahead up the stone steps, or turn left along what was formerly a main street, still with its original paving. Both lead to the town centre at the top of the hill. At its heart was the palace, smaller than but similar in style to Knossos and Malia. It was probably the seat of the local governor.

To the south, L-shaped stairs lead to a large courtyard that was the agora, or market-place. The large stone slab next to the stairs may have been a sacrificial altar (or simply a butcher's block). To the north was the sanctuary, where a shrine with snake-goddess figures and other cult objects was found.

As you survey the site from the top of the acropolis remember that Gournia was four times larger than what you see today. Imagine it stretching northward all the way to the sea, as it did in antiquity.

TAKING A BREAK

There are **no refreshments** at Gournia, so bring your own water and snacks.

A maze of streets and steps at Gournia

➕ 185 E3 ☎ 28420-93028 🕐 Daily 8:30–3 🚌 Buses from Agios Nikolaos to Sitia and Ierapetra can drop you near the site 💷 Inexpensive ❓ Photography allowed

GOURNIA: INSIDE INFO

Top tips Save for a couple of small trees, **there is no shade.** Wear sunblock, hat and sunglasses for protection.
■ Gournia is **delightful in springtime** when colourful wild flowers blossom amid the stones.

Getting there The **turning off the National Highway** (New Road) is easy to miss. Driving east, a few kilometres beyond Istro start to look for the sign for Gournia, just beyond, on a sudden right turn on to a gravel road.

5 Sitia

If for no other reason, visit Sitia for the magnificent drive that takes you there through some of the finest scenery on Crete. Beyond Agios Nikolaos the National Highway becomes a high cliff road that winds up and down the mountainsides with tantalising glimpses of the sea. Once in Sitia, you'll be delighted by its atmosphere. Set around a beautiful bay, it's more laid-back town than tourist resort and makes an excellent base from which to explore the attractions of the far eastern end of the island.

Crete's fifth largest town sits on the western side of the pretty Bay of Sitia, its sun-bleached houses climbing up the hillside above the waterfront. A wide promenade curves along the harbour, shaded by squat palms and backed by a ring of pleasant tavernas that provide the perfect spot to chill out and watch the colourful fishing boats bobbing on the water. East of the marina, just beyond the tourist office, is the sandy town beach. Although tourism is growing, locals outnumber tourists here.

There is much history here. Remains of a substantial Minoan settlement were discovered in the southern suburb of Petras, and more Minoan villas and peak sanctuaries were found in this region of Crete than anywhere else. West of the harbour towards the ferry port are the remains of Roman fish tanks. On the eastern outskirts of town the ruins of Hellenistic Sitia are under excavation.

Earthquakes destroyed the town's Venetian-era buildings,

The ancient Hellenistic site of Tripitos

save for the fortress that stands out on the hilltop. It is now used as an open-air theatre, particularly during the town's cultural festival, the **Kornaria**, held in July and August (➤ 124).

Archaeology Museum

This small but excellent museum contains many treasures from eastern Crete dating from neolithic to Roman times. The first section contains finds from various sites in Minoan Sitia. More than 80 excavated sites indicate the density of settlement in this region. Many beautiful pieces of pottery were discovered in cemeteries and their decoration is outstanding both in quality and preservation. In case 7 an exquisite figure of a bull comes from the cemetery at Mochlos. Crete's best-preserved hieroglyphic archive was discovered at Petras and there are examples in case 27.

Next come exhibits from the Zakros Palati (➤ 118), which yielded many unusual finds. The decoration on the large *pithoi* (storage jars) is superb. There are rare fragments of Linear A tablets, remarkably well preserved due to a cataclysmic fire that acted like a kiln and baked the clay. Another case holds beautiful rounded pitchers, three-legged pots, tiny vases and curious kitchen utensils, including a terracotta grill.

Post-Minoan-era finds complete the collection. Case 22 holds odd votive objects from an archaic sanctuary: the clay Egyptian-style heads were inserted into phial-shaped bodies, and may have been associated with fertility rites. In the last room a water tank contains a mass of vases compacted in a Roman shipwreck.

Left: Peace by the harbour at Sitia

EROTÓKRITOS

Vitsentzos Kornáros, author of the epic poem *Erotókritos*, was born in Sitia in the 17th century. Standing on the waterfront by the tourist office is a monument to him, with scenes from his work, which is still sung today (➤ 14).

Folk Museum

Sitia also has a charming little folk museum, set in a former upper-class house. There are displays of agricultural tools, kitchen implements and a century-old loom, plus fine examples of traditional bedspreads, embroidery and other handiwork. Be sure to go upstairs to see the decorative 1890 bridal bed with silk canopy and coverings.

On the Outskirts

Sitia is one of Crete's best wine producing regions and a **wine co-operative** on the main road into town gives wine tours in summer. This includes a video on the wine-making process, a look around the museum and a tasting of local wines and olive oil, both of which are for sale.

About 2km (1 mile) along the beach road, heading east towards Vai, a signed track on the left marked "Archaeological Site" leads to the Hellenistic site of Tripitos, which dates from the 3rd century BC. Park beside the farm building and walk up to the fenced site, which you can enter. The site is still under excavation, but the foundations of many buildings, rooms and streets are visible, and there's a grand view over the sea.

TAKING A BREAK

You're spoiled for choice along the waterfront. **Kolios** is a good spot for breakfast; **O Mixos** (➤ 122) for a meal.

➕ 186 B3

Archaeology Museum
✉ Odos Eleftherias Venizelou, opposite the bus station ☎ 28430-23917
🕐 Tue–Sun 8:30–3 💷 Inexpensive ❓ No flash photography

Folk Museum
✉ Kapetan Sifi 26 ☎ 28430-22861 🕐 Apr–Oct Mon 9:30–1:30, 5–8, Tue–Fri 9:30–2:30, 5–9, Sat 9:30–2:30 💷 Inexpensive ❓ Photography allowed

Wine Co-operative
✉ Missonos 74 ☎ 28430-25200 🕐 Mon–Fri 8:30–2:30; www.sitiacoop.gr 💷 Free

Restaurants line Sitia's waterfront

SITIA: INSIDE INFO

Top tip Sitia's **waterfront** is so pleasant and relaxing that you may find yourself spending an extra day in the town.

One to miss The **ruins of the Roman fish tanks** are largely submerged and almost impossible to make out.

At Your Leisure

6 North Coast Resorts

Chersonisou (⊞ 184 B4) is the biggest and brashest of the northeast coast resorts. It's synonymous with raucous, alcohol-fuelled nightlife and most people come here to party. The main road, 2km (1 mile) long,

---

FOR CHILDREN
Ideon Dikteon (➤ 114)
Spinalonga Island (➤ 115)
Gournia(➤ 108–109)
Makrygialos and **Paralia Vaies** (➤ 114, 117)

---

and parallel beach road are packed solid with bars, shops and services, joined by narrow side streets crammed with hotels. But where's the beach? The narrow patches of sand are largely hidden among the hotels and the rocky coastline. A port (*limín*) in antiquity, the resort is also called Limenas Chersonisou to distinguish it from the village of "Old" Chersonisou that lies slightly inland. A few kilometres east is **Malia**

A quiet stretch of the beach at Malia

(⊞ 184 C4), the north coast's other famous party resort. It's just as busy and noisy but mildly more attractive. The sandy beaches, about a kilometre from the main road, can get crowded – those to the east are quieter. Malia Palace (➤ 102–103) lies just beyond Tropical Beach. The old village is uphill on the opposite side of the main road, with good traditional tavernas along its winding streets and in its pretty square.

In between the two is **Stalida** (⊞ 184 C4), or **Stalis**, a burgeoning, tightly packed resort with a sandy beach and quieter nightlife. West of Chersonisou you'll find the smaller resorts of **Chani Kokkini** (⊞ 184 A4) and **Kato Gouves** (⊞ 184 B4).

7 Dikteon Andron

Located high in the Dikti Mountains above the village of Psichro, this is the most famous and impressive cave on Crete. In mythology it is said to be the birthplace of the god Zeus (➤ 91), and its importance as a cult centre since Minoan times was confirmed by the discovery of a huge number of votive offerings. It remained a place of religious ritual for the Dorian Greeks long after the Minoans' demise.

From the car park it's a 15-minute uphill walk to the entrance, but in summer donkey rides are on offer if you don't fancy the climb. The 65m (213 feet) descent into the depths of the cave has been made easier, if less mysterious, by concrete steps and lighting. The path circles around the bottom, alongside a dark pool, with views of the great stalactites and stalagmites. It takes a little imagination to pick out such features as the "nipples" where the baby god suckled, but with the cave's mouth a mere slit of light far above, you can sense the mystical wonder it held for the ancient Cretans. This is especially true if you beat the crowds by visiting early morning or late afternoon.

➕ 184 C3 ⏰ Daily 8–7 🍴 Café (€)
🅿 Moderate; additional parking fee

The market town of Neapoli

8 Neapoli

Tourists largely overlook this market town, but it has much local charm. The roads end at the main square next to the large, modern church. On the south side of the square a small **folklore museum** has local artefacts recalling the traditional way of life. Opposite the war memorial, the café **I Driros** is the place to sample the local speciality – a sweet, milky drink called *soumádha*, made from pressed almonds. It's also a pleasant spot from which to observe the passing scene.

Neapoli makes a good base for exploring the Lasithiou Plateau (➤ 160–162). Odos Ethnikis Antistasis leads from the square to

SOUTH COAST BEACHES

There are several beaches along Crete's southeast coast. **Makrygialos** and **Analipsi** have merged into one large, rather unattractive resort, but the beach is sandy and the water very shallow. Further west, **Agia Fotia** is a small, somewhat hidden place with a fine beach.

the town's only hotel, the Neapolis
(➤ 120).

➕ 185 D4 🚍 Buses from Agios Nikolaos
and Malia

🗎 Elounda

Situated about 7km (4 miles) north
of Agios Nikolaos, on the western
shores of the Gulf of Mirabello,
Elounda is a pretty and much more
low-key resort than its neighbour.
The long main road through town
leads to a large square set around
the harbour, which, lined with cafés
and restaurants, is the focal point
of activity. Boat trips to Spinalonga
Island leave regularly from here. Just
beyond the parking area is the sandy
town beach.

Spinalonga Island's Venetian fortress

🔟 Spinalonga

A short boat ride from Elounda
brings you to the eeriest place
on Crete, tiny Spinalonga Island,
commanding the entrance to the
bay. The Venetians built a fortress
here in 1579 to defend the gulf and
it remained one of the island's most
formidable strongholds long after the
Turkish invasion, only handed over
by treaty in 1715. Turkish settlers
built homes here and refused to leave
after Greece won independence. The
government persuaded them to go
by designating Spinalonga a leper
colony in 1903. It was the last of its
kind in Europe, and existed until it
was evacuated in 1957.

From boat to table – Elounda's catch
quickly makes its way to your plate

   On the southern edge of town
– reached by a small road along
the shore that passes Venetian
salt pans – is a causeway. It runs
above a submerged isthmus that
once connected the mainland to
Spinalonga Peninsula. From here,
when the waters are calm, you can
see a few remains of the sunken
city of **Olous**. Behind the taverna
on the causeway a fenced area
protects the black and white
mosaic floor of a 4th-century
church. There are good
beaches and birding on
the peninsula.

➕ 185 E4 🚍 Bus from Agios
Nikolaos 🍴 Small kiosk by
the car park at the harbour
square(€)

   The approach to the island is
stunning, with the reflections of
the round keep of the fortress
and its walls gleaming in the bay.
Sometimes, guides meet you on
shore to tell the sad tale of life on the
"island of the living dead", as it was
locally known. There are wonderful
views from the ramparts.

➕ 185 E4 🕐 Boats daily in season, every 30
minutes 9:30–4:30 💶 Expensive (for boat)

⑪ Ierapetra

With Africa just 300km (186 miles) away, Ierapetra is Europe's southernmost city. Though it gets the most sunshine, too, its prosperity comes not from tourism but from the farmers who grow year-round crops of tomatoes and peppers in masses of plastic greenhouses along this coast.

The only attractive part of this sprawling town – the fourth largest on Crete and the biggest on the south coast – is the waterfront area near the Venetian fort. You can wander around inside its ramshackle ramparts though there's not much to see. Near by is a bell tower and the red-tiled domes of a 14th-century church, Afentis Christos. Some characterful houses still stand in the winding lanes of the old Turkish quarter, behind the waterfront. Seek out the small square with an ornate Ottoman fountain and a restored Turkish mosque.

The small **Archaeology Museum** has two particular treasures: a 2nd-century statue of Demeter, goddess of fertility, holding an ear of corn; and a Minoan *larnax*, or lidded clay coffin, with superb decoration depicting a wild goat hunt and other figures. A morning fruit market is held near the museum.

Ierapetra looks south to Africa

A long, sandy beach stretches west of town, or take a boat trip to the more appealing beaches of **Chrysi Island**, 12km (7 miles) offshore.
➕ 185 E2 (Archaeology Museum, tel: 28422-8721) 🕐 Tue–Sun 8:30–3 💵 Inexpensive

⑫ Mirtos

The appeal of this charming south coast village far outweighs its small size. There are no sights, save a two-room local museum, and its long grey sand beach is not outstanding,

Getting the daily bread at Mirtos

but it's the sort of place where people drop in for a day and end up staying for months. Perhaps it's because Mirtos remains a village, rather than a resort, and the tourists who come here prefer to blend into the local scene. The pleasant tavernas along the waterfront make a delightful stop.
➕ 185 D2 🚌 Bus from Ierapetra

🔢 Moni Toplou

Alone on a small windy hilltop, Moni Toplou looks more like a fortress than a monastery. In reality, it was. Its name means "cannon" in Turkish, and artillery was installed here in Venetian times after it was sacked by pirates in 1498. Thus began its long history as a centre of resistance (➤ 19).

Toplou owns much of the surrounding land and is said to be one of the richest monasteries in Greece. Its grounds and buildings have been greatly restored. Outside the entrance is an old stone windmill; look inside to see how the huge wooden millstones were turned by the sails to grind flour.

Inside the walls, the pretty cobbled courtyard – bright with flowers and greenery – is surrounded by the monks' cells and the bell tower. The church holds the monastery's great treasure: an 18th-century icon by Ioánnis Kornáros entitled *Lord, Thou Art Great*. It comprises 61 intricate biblical scenes, each illustrating a line from this Greek Orthodox prayer, and is considered a masterpiece of Cretan art. More icons can be seen in the museum and one room highlights the monastery's role in the battle for Cretan independence and during World War II.

🚩 186 B3 ☎ 28430-61226 🕐 Daily 9–1, 2–6 💰 Moderate ❓ Photography limited

🔢 Paralia Vai

Although the crowds that flock to Crete's famous palm beach can mar the idyllic environment they've come to see, it's still worth a visit especially off-season when you'll be alone. For the most scenic approach, take the road that passes Moni Toplou rather than the one through Palaikastro. As you descend through the stark landscape reminiscent of North Africa, a forest of date palms suddenly rises up oasis-like before you. *Phoenix theophrasti* is unique to eastern Crete, the last of a palm species that was once widespread in the southeast Aegean. Some say the grove grew from date stones spat out by Egyptian soldiers who camped here, others that the date-eaters were pirates. The grove covers 20 hectares (50 acres) in a narrow valley stretching to the beach. Tour buses call in here during summer, when the wide sandy beach is generally packed for much of the day. It quietens down around 4pm, so come early or late in the day to appreciate its beauty.

🚩 186 C4 🍴 Café (€) 🚌 Buses from Sitia and Makrygialos 🅿 Parking inexpensive, beach free

Looking down at Paralia Vai

🔢 Zakros Palati

If you make time to visit the fourth of Crete's great Minoan palaces, at the remote eastern reaches of the island, you'll be well rewarded. From Sitia the winding road takes you across a beautiful high plateau ringed by mountains. Allow an hour (minimum) to get to the ancient site, which lies 8km (5 miles) beyond Ano Zakros (the upper town) at sea-level Kato Zakros. Here a few pleasant tavernas face an idyllic pebble beach.

Built around 1900 BC, Zakros had a fine harbour and was the island's main naval base, flourishing on trade with Egypt and the Middle East. Like the other great Minoan palaces, it too was destroyed by catastrophic events around 1450 BC.

However, because the site was so isolated it had never been looted and when it was excavated in the 1960s more than 10,000 artefacts were found, many of them unique. Magnificent ivory, bronze and stoneware, including elaborate vases and chalices, are now in the museums at Iraklio and Sitia.

The dig yielded another remarkable find: in a ritual well filled with spring water the archaeologists discovered a votive cup of olives some 3,000 years old. Before the olives could disintegrate, the crew bravely tasted them – and found them as delicious as if they had just been picked.

Though Zakros is similar in design to the other palaces, it is far more peaceful and atmospheric. To the west of the central court and banquet hall is the central shrine, an archive where hundreds of Linear A tablets were stored, and the treasury where the famous rock crystal *rhyton* (► 52) was found.

Surveying the Palace from Ano Zakros (the Upper Town)

The large round cistern, like the other wells, is full of terrapins. Beyond this, under a canopy, is a bathroom where visitors might have washed before entering the court. You can see the basins and traces of red fresco.

Large stone steps lead to the exit, which was the original entrance to the palace from the harbour road. Rising up the hillside are the ruins of the Upper Town, which afford great views over the entire site.

🚩 186 C3 ☎ 28430-61204
🕐 Daily 8:30–3 (last entrance 2:30) 🚌 Bus from Sitia
💰 Inexpensive

Where to... Stay

Prices

Prices are for a double room per night in high season including taxes

€ under €70   €€ €70–€150   €€€ over €150

AGIOS NIKOLAOS

Coral Hotel €€

The Coral, right on the waterfront, is the slightly less expensive sister hotel to the Hermes (see below), which has a fitness centre that guests here can use. Try to get one of the sea-view rooms, although all have bath, fridge, air-conditioning, phone and radio. There is a meeting room. The hotel has its own restaurant, with a sea view, and a rooftop swimming pool. It lays on a substantial breakfast buffet.

✚ 185 D3 ☒ Akti Koundourou, Agios Nikolaos ☎ 28410-22058; www.hermes-hotels.gr ⏲ Apr–Oct

Hermes Hotel €€€

Along the waterfront from the Coral (see left), this smart hotel has a stylish lobby with a shop, flagstone floors and a wall lined with large copies of frescoes from Knossos. Here all the 200 rooms and six suites are spacious and have satellite TV, radio, phone, fridge and hairdryers, making it one of the most comfortable bases in the centre of town. In addition, the Hermes has a restaurant, a rooftop pool, a fitness centre and easy access to a diving club nearby (▶ 124).

✚ 185 D3 ☒ Akti Koundourou, Agios Nikolaos ☎ 28410-28253; www.hermes-hotels.gr

Istron Bay €€€

One of the best hotels on the island the Istron, some 12km (7 miles) east of Agios Nikolaos, overlooks its own beach and a beautiful bay. Built into the cliff, all rooms have large balconies with sea views.

They are good-sized and decorated in traditional blue and white. The restaurant has won awards for its gourmet cooking, and with its own swimming pool and friendly service the hotel is popular, so book ahead.

✚ 185 D3 ☒ Istro, Agios Nikolaos ☎ 28410-61303; www.istronbay.com ⏲ Apr–Oct

Minos Beach Art Hotel €€€

If your idea of a holiday is lounging on a sun bed within splashing distance of the sea or diving from the rocks into the crystal clear ocean, then the Minos Beach Art Hotel will more than satisfy. Set in shady gardens of olive groves and eucalypts, right on the water's edge, this low-rise resort of stylish white minimalist bungalows is ideal for a barefoot holiday. Opt for a VIP bungalow or executive suite for sea views from your private terrace. The hotel boasts several excellent eateries, spa and fitness facilities.

✚ 185 D3 ☒ Outskirts of Agios Nikolaos, 72100 ☎ 28410-22345; www.slh.com/minosbeach

ELOUNDA

Elounda Bay Palace €€€

Overlooking the turquoise waters of beautiful Mirabello Bay and set in aromatic Mediterranean gardens, this luxurious resort makes for a languorous escape. There's a sandy beach, but the swimming pool is hard to leave, especially if you book a villa room with a private pool. If you are feeling more active, there's a golf course and access to water sports and scuba-diving, and Six Senses Spa is close by. Rooms are spacious with polished floorboards, DVD players and internet access.

✚ 185 E4 ☒ Elounda Bay ☎ 28410 67000; www.lhw.com/EloundaBayPalace

Elounta Beach €€€

This small, luxury resort, with some 260 rooms including de luxe suites that each have their own private little swimming pool, can claim to be the best hotel on Crete. Needless to say, the rooms have everything, including lots of space. If the TV is not enough you can borrow a video. There are numerous restaurants and bars, every indoor and outdoor facility you could wish for, and a breakfast buffet that could see you through the day.

🚪 185 D4 ⊠ Elounda ☎ 08410-41412; www.eloundabeach.gr ⏱ Apr–Oct

Eloundha Mare €€€

One of the best hotels on the island, this deluxe resort overlooks the Mirabello Gulf. In addition to its regular rooms, it has luxury villas, each with its own private swimming pool. Rooms are decorated in a style that mixes traditional wooden furniture with lots of marble and, of course, all modern amenties. There are three restaurants, golf, tennis,

watersports galore, and it is well placed for visiting both Elounta and Agios Nikolaos.

🚪 185 E4 ⊠ Elounta ☎ 28410-41102; www.elounda.com ⏱ Apr–Oct

KATO ZAKROS

Bay View Apartments €

Easily spotted by the profusion of plants around, they command stunning views of the surrounding area and the sea. The rooms have bright, white walls and although extremely simple are clean and comfortable with TV, fridge, ensuite facilities and lovely verandas to relax on: a terrific bargain.

🚪 186 C2 ⊠ Kato Zakros ☎ 28430-26887

MIRTOS

Hotel Myrtos €

Probably the best of a limited range of accommodation in Mirtos, this inexpensive hotel is right in the packed centre of this little town, with its own restaurant attached.

The rooms are a decent size with basic facilities, and a small balcony runs around the outside of the building, which all rooms can enjoy. Air conditioning costs extra

🚪 185 D2 ⊠ Mirtos ☎ 28420-51227; www.myrtoshotel.com

NEAPOLI

Neapolis Hotel €

An eye-catching art deco-style building, the Neapolis has 12 basic rooms fitted out with stripped-pine furniture. All the rooms have small balconies overlooking the street (though noise is not a problem in this charming hill town) and some have air-conditioning. The breakfast is generous, often with fresh fruit added for good measure You may return at night to find old men playing cards in the lobby, or the local priest watching the TV. Charming and well maintained, the hotel offers excellent value.

🚪 185 D4 ⊠ Evagelistrias Platia, Neapoli ☎ 28410-33967

SITIA

Elysée €€€

Right on the waterfront, the Elysée is a short stroll from the beach and the centre. The rooms are clean and simple; those at the front have balconies with views over the harbour, and all have fridge, TV and phone. There is a breakfast room and a small lounge, plus ample private parking behind the hotel.

🚪 186 B3 ⊠ Karamanli 14, Sitia ☎ 28430-22312

Itanos Hotel €

This family hotel has 72 rooms in a building by the main square and overlooking the waterfront. The rooms are standard for this price range, and all have phone, satellite TV, radio, bath, air-conditioning, balconies and soundproof doors. Try to get a room at the front for the sea views. There is a large dining room and bar, and a patisserie.

🚪 186 B3 ⊠ Karamanli, 4, Sitia ☎ 28430-22901; www.dilos.com/hotel/501

Where to...
Eat and Drink

Prices

Prices are for a two-course meal for one person, excluding drinks and tips

€ under €20   €€ €20–€40   €€€ €40

AGIOS NIKOLAOS

Barko €€€

This elegant fine-dining restaurant overlooking lovely Kitroplatia Beach is a rarity in Crete and is widely acknowledged as being the best in Agios Nikolaos. The chef serves up refined Cretan dishes with a creative twist, often combining unexpected ingredients and flavours with flair to produce exquisitely presented plates and truly memorable meals. Order Cretan wine from the impressive list and enjoy the warmth of the room and friendly service. If you're here on a weekend, you'll need to reserve a table in advance. Do as the locals do, and dress up for the occasion.

➕ 185 D3 ✉ Agios Nikolaos ☎ 28410-24610 ⏰ Daily, lunch & dinner; weekends only in winter

Meltemi €€€

Hotel restaurants sometimes disappoint, but the Meltemi at the Istron Bay (▶ 119) is exceptional. It is one of the best eateries on the island and has won awards for its imaginative cuisine ranging from seafood to hearty but subtle meat dishes. You can also opt for the nightly buffet, which allows you to choose from a good selection of hot and cold Greek dishes. There is an extensive wine list, too. Non-residents are welcome in the stylish dining room that overlooks the sea. Booking is advised.

➕ 185 D3 ✉ Istro, Agios Nikolaos ☎ 28410-61303/61347 ⏰ Apr–Oct Mon–Wed, Fri–Sat 7pm–10.30pm

La Strada €

One of the town's few good restaurants to stay open all year, La Strada is deservedly popular with the locals. The long menu may put you off – after all, how could a restaurant do so many dishes well? Yet La Strada pulls it off, serving up hearty home-cooked Greek and Cretan fare alongside tasty Italian pastas and good pizzas. If you're opting for Greek, the mixed *mezedes* plate is wonderful way to begin the meal (it takes a long time for a reason!) and traditional Greek dishes such as *stifado* and *kleftiko* are great choice for mains. The restaurant offers free transport to/from your hotel.

➕ 185 D3 ✉ Odos Plastira, Agios Nikolaos ☎ 28410 25524 ⏰ Daily, all day

Pelagos €€

A fishing boat and a beautiful shady palm-filled courtyard where the tables stand on a stone floor identifies Pelagos. Inside there are several small, intimate rooms with bright blue and yellow paintwork. Food is served all day although you are welcome to sit just for a drink and a nibble. Seafood is the speciality, including octopus, mussels and of course the catch of the day, but meat-lovers and vegetarians are also well catered for.

➕ 185 D3 ✉ Koraka/Katechaki 10, Agios Niklaos ☎ 28410-25737 ⏰ Apr–Oct daily noon–midnight

ELOUNDA

Ferryman's Taverna €€

Hearty home-cooked Cretan cuisine distinguishes the Ferryman, one of several restaurants at the southern end of the Elounda waterfront. In appearance it is much like the others, with outdoor seating overlooking the water and a bar across the street. The cooking here is of a high standard. Among the most popular dishes are Cretan lamb in red wine and a pork dish cooked with bacon, mushrooms, garlic, white wine and fresh cream. The bar opens for light meals and *mezedes* out of season.

🏠 185 E4 ⊠ Elounda ☎ 28410-41230
⊕ Apr–Oct daily 10am–late

Vritomartes €€

This unmissable seafood restaurant stands out on the breakwater with its name emblazoned on the side in letters feet high. A pleasant seating area overlooks the water, and before you get there you pass the tank containing live fish and lobsters. Make your choice of these if you are going for seafood. However, the menu is not confined to seafood, and it would be a shame not to try the more imaginative dishes, even if they push the price up a little.

🏠 185 E4 ⊠ G Sfiraki waterfront, Elounda ☎ 08410-41325 ⊕ Apr–Oct daily 10am–11pm

Kato Zakros Bay Restaurant €

This family taverna is right by the sea. In addition to the indoor seating there are pleasant tables outside overlooking the beach. The restaurant owners breed rabbit, quail and grouse; the vegetables come from their own garden; and all meals are cooked in local olive oil… and it shows in the results.

🏠 186 C2 ⊠ Kato Zakros ☎ 28430-26887
⊕ Apr–Oct daily all day

Taverna Akti €€

At the far eastern end of the string of waterfront tavernas, the Akti is one of the oldest and best restaurants in Mirtos. Outdoor tables with blue and white checked tablecloths overlook the beach, and there is plenty of indoor seating. The friendly owner offers various specialities, including charcoal-cooked meats and fresh fish. One special dish is the octopus *stifado*.

🏠 185 D2 ⊠ Mirtos ☎ 08420-51584
⊕ Apr–Nov daily 10am–late

The Cretan House €€

Set along the waterfront near the beach, this large restaurant is a favourite with both locals and visitors alike. The large outdoor terrace is the perfect place for catching the sea breezes, but the inside is equally delightful. Artefacts decorate the walls, while above the bar is a re-creation of a traditional Cretan kitchen. Fresh fish naturally features, but try the range of home-made Cretan specialities too.

🏠 186 B3 ⊠ Karamanli 10, Sitia
☎ 28430-25133 ⊕ Daily 10am–late

O Mixos €€

Here waiters race back and forth with orders and dishes between the main seating area down on the waterfront and the back-street kitchen. The quality of the food is superb, with an emphasis on meat and fish grilled on charcoal, cooked outside in the traditional way. Oven-baked dishes also feature, with lamb and artichoke casserole one speciality of the house.

🏠 186 B3 ⊠ Kornarou 117, Sitia
☎ 28430-22416 ⊕ Daily 10am–late

Il Palazzo €

It is surprising to find an Italian restaurant in a Greek hill village, let alone one as enjoyable as this. This is very much a family affair. The authentic pizzas, cooked in the oven in the dining room, are excellent. There is a lovely covered patio area out at the front, with a flagstone floor and potted plants along the outer wall.

🏠 185 D4 ⊠ I Sergaki 14, Neapoli
☎ 28410-34180 ⊕ Daily 6pm–late

Where to... Shop

Agios Nikolaos has the most varied shopping in eastern Crete. Pedestrianised Odos 28 Oktovriou is largely geared for tourists, with restaurants and souvenir shops. There are more shops along Roussou Koundourou and Stakiaraki streets. All round the harbour and lake area numerous jewellery shops sell both modern and antique designs.

TEXTILES AND LOCAL CRAFTS

Just 10km (6 miles) away from Agios Nikolaos, the mountain village of **Kritsa** is famous for its textiles. Here the streets are literally draped with rugs, wall hangings, woven bags, embroidered tablecloths and other traditional handicrafts. Make sure you purchase genuine handmade articles (▶ 95). These will usually be more expensive but higher in quality.

The villages around the **Diktaean Cave** on the Lasithiou Plateau, particularly **Psychro**, also have a lot of textiles for sale. On the outskirts of **Zenia** (▶ 160) look for the elderly spoon-carver selling his wares outside his house. They're solid and finely crafted and they make a unique and authentic gift and it's a charming place to stop and watch him work.

Surprisingly for a provincial town, **Neapoli** has several modern gift shops with unusual and attractive items. These are on Odos Ethnikis Antistasis, the main street into town between the Neapolis Hotel and the main square. The shop at No 56 sells traditional Cretan items, such as bells for goats and sheep in various sizes with or without the leather collar; also baskets, knives, carved walking sticks, wooden spoons and forks, and traditional high boots.

ICONS

Eastern Crete is a good area to shop for traditional Greek icons. The gift shop opposite **Panagia Kera**, just outside Kritsa (▶ 104–105), has some lovely and authentic handpainted icons. They're not inexpensive, but the price reflects the skill and time involved in producing high-quality artwork. Beautifully painted icons, at better prices, can be found at the **Petrakis Icon Workshop** in Elounda (tel: 28410-41669/41461). It is open Apr–Oct daily 10am–11pm; phone for hours in winter.

BOOKS

Opposite Petrakis, tucked between the waterfront and the main road in Elounda, is **Eklektos**, a good bookshop which sells not only maps and guides but also fiction, poetry and essays on all things Cretan – and in several languages. There is also a huge second-hand section for paperbacks, plus top-quality gifts such as stationery, crystals and clothing (open Apr–Oct daily 10am–10:30pm; tel: 28410-41641).

MARKETS

Every Wednesday morning an outdoor market next to the main hospital at **Agios Nikolaos** sells food, produce and clothes. **Ierapetra** has a street market on Saturday mornings by the Proto Yimmasio (first high school) and **Sitia** on Tuesdays on Odos Plastira. Markets generally close around 1pm. Cheese from the **Lasithiou** and **Katharo plateaux** is especially good; try the *graviera*. Sitia is a major wine-producing area – the red wines are very popular.

Where to...
Be Entertained

NIGHTLIFE

Eastern Crete's north coast resorts are the nightlife capital of the island. In **Limenas Chersonisou** and **Malia**, bars and nightclubs buzz all night long. Among the most popular venues in Chersonisou are **Aria**, one of the biggest discos on Crete; and **Status**, **New York**, **Mouragio** and **Camelot Club** near the waterfront. On the main road is the **Fame Bar**, with soul, funk and jazz music; **Palace of Dance 99**; and **Cheers**, both of which often have live music. Malia's most popular party is **Zoo**. Other hotspots on the beach road include **Zig Zag's**, **Apollo** and **Babylon**. The **R&B Dance Club** is a fun place to spend a night.

One of the largest dance clubs in Agios Nikolaos is **Lipstick**, but there are lively bars in the centre.

Along Sitia's waterfront are popular music bars such as **Nea Glyfada**, **Scala**, **Club Porto** and **Albatros**. Larger discos include **Hot Summer** on the beach road, and **Planitarion**, west of the ferry port.

TRADITIONAL MUSIC AND FESTIVALS

The tavernas around the square in **Malia** old town often stage live Greek music, and in summer frequent performances of Cretan music and dance take place at the **Lychnostatis Open-Air Museum**, on the eastern edge of Chersonisou. **Sitia** is also the site of several cultural events. The main festival,

the **Kornaria** (June or July to mid-August), features folklore dances, popular music, village feasts and exhibitions. Performances take place in the old Venetian fortress, or in the town square. Details available from the tourist office (▶ 37).

The **Sultanina** (Wine Festival) follows the Kornaria, a four-day event marking the beginning of the grape harvest in mid-August with traditional music and dance. In winter, the **Carnival** is held at the fortress on the last Sunday before Lent. A bulletin listing events is distributed around town in summer.

Agios Nikolaos holds a cultural festival, the **Lato** (June to September), with theatre, concerts, dance and festival events. Details from the tourist office (▶ 37).

SPORTS

The north coast beach resorts offer a wide range of **water sports**. **Water City** (tel: 2810-781317; www.watercity.gr), Crete's biggest

waterpark, is just inland from Kokkini Hani. Limenas Chersonisou has two more waterparks: **AquaPlus** (tel: 28970-24950) and **Star Beach** (tel: 28970-24434). All are open daily in summer (times vary). You can try **go-karting** at **Kartland** (tel: 28970-32769), next to Star Beach.

Agios Nikolaos is good for **scuba diving**. Dive centres are strictly controlled and offer lessons and equipment rental. PADI-certified centres include **Creta's Happy Divers** (tel: 28410-82546) opposite the Coral Hotel; **Pelagos Diving Centre** (tel: 28410-22345/24376) at Minos Beach Hotel; and the diving centre at the **Istron Bay Hotel** (▶ 119). Diving is also offered at **Vai Beach** (July–September).

The **Municipal Beach Club** at Agios Nikolaos (daily 9am–late) has mini-golf, billiards, table tennis, life-size chess and a basketball court, as well as watersports.

RiX Outdoor Activities (tel: 28410-82231) offers **bicycle** and **skate** rentals and numerous **tours**.

Western Crete

Getting Your Bearings

From the two loveliest cities on the north coast to the biggest gorge in Europe, which plunges down from the central mountains to the southern sea, western Crete has some of the island's best features. These include the two most historically interesting monasteries on Crete, Arkadiou in the north and Preveli in the south, both of which played immense roles in the island's battles for independence.

Chania and Rethymno, Crete's second and third largest cities respectively, have fine restaurants, museums and Venetian history. But if your only view of western Crete is of these busy parts of the north coast, you'll see just a fraction of what the area has to offer. The beaches here are bustling, and some resorts such as Platanias and Bali are packed with summer sun-worshippers. But head south into the White Mountains (Lefka Ori), the island's highest and most dramatic range, and that world immediately disappears, to be replaced by quiet villages and breathtaking views.

Many people undertake the day-long trek through the Samaria Gorge, one of the most exciting experiences on the island, but other gorges, such as the Impros Gorge, also make for great walks. These are largely found along the south coast, which

is much more rugged than the north. Options here range from hidden backwaters like Sougia to growing resorts such as Palaiochora.

To the west are inland hill villages surrounded by orchards, while down by the sea you'll find remote beaches, including the popular but still gorgeous sands of Elafonisi. Spend at least a day driving around this region to take in some of western Crete's spectacular beauty.

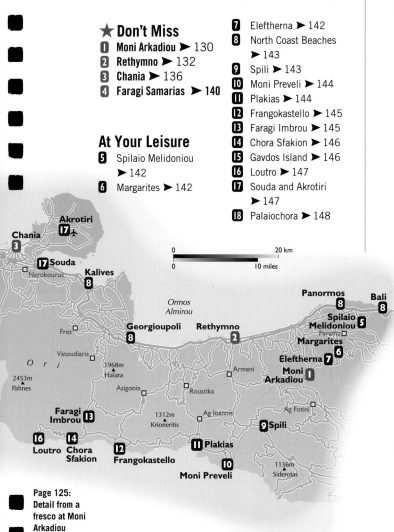

Akrotiri
17

Chania
3

17 Souda
Nerokouros
Kalives
8

Ormos
Almirou

Fres

Vatoudiaris

Georgioupoli
8

Rethymno
2

Panormos
8

Bali
8

Spilaio
Melidoniou 5
Perama
Margarites 6
Eleftherna 7
Moni
Arkadiou 1

O r i
2453m
Pahnes
1968m
Halara
Asigonia
Armeni
Roustika

Ag Ioannis
Ag Fotini

Faragi
Imbrou 13
1312m
Krioneritis

9 Spili

16
Loutro
14
Chora
Sfakion
12
Frangokastello
11 Plakias
10
Moni Preveli
1136m
Siderotas

0   20 km
0   10 miles

Page 125:
Detail from a
fresco at Moni
Arkadiou

Left: Mosaic
in Chania's
Archeological
Museum

Right: Monks
still live in the
monastery of
Preveli

In Five Days

If you're not quite sure where to begin your travels, this itinerary recommends a practical and enjoyable five-day tour of Western Crete, taking in some of the best places to see using the Getting Your Bearings map on the previous page. For more information see the main entries.

Day One

Morning
Explore **1 Moni Arkadiou** (icon, right, ➤ 130–131) then take the pleasant country road (signposted at the end of the car park) to the ancient site of **7 Eleftherna** (➤ 142). Continue on to the potters' village of **6 Margarites** (➤ 142). Have lunch in Margarites. Taverna Gianousakis at the upper end of the village is a pleasant place with good home-cooked food.

Afternoon
Drive northeast to visit the **5 Spilaio Melidoniou** (➤ 142), then continue north to the coast road, perhaps stopping for a swim at one of the north coast beaches on your way west to Rethymno.

Evening
Spend the night at **2 Rethymno** (left, ➤ 132–135). For dinner, sample the food at Myrogdies and enjoy the live music, too (➤ 152).

Day Two

Morning/Lunch
Explore Rethymno, perhaps spending the morning at the museums and art gallery, or at the Fortezza. Don't miss a meal at the Avli (➤ 152).

Afternoon
Explore the narrow streets of the old town, see the loggia, stroll around the Venetian harbour and visit the public gardens.

Evening
Enjoy a relaxing meal by the sea, but instead of choosing one of the touristy restaurants by the inner harbour, go to the Cavo d'Oro (➤ 152).

Day Three

Morning/Lunch
Drive south to **10 Moni Preveli** (► 144), the last stretch through dramatic gorge scenery. Head west through **11 Plakias** (► 144) and along the narrow, winding coastal road to **12 Frangokastello** (► 145). Dine by the lovely little harbour at **14 Chora Sfakion** (► 146). The Livikon Restaurant, the town's oldest, serves good Cretan specialities.

Afternoon
Drive north past the **13 Faragi Imbrou** (► 145). You can occasionally glimpse the chasm from the road, even if you have no time to walk it. Head for Chania, stopping off at the Allied War Cemetery near **17 Souda** (► 147–148) if time permits.

Evening
Spend three nights in **Chania** (lighthouse, right, ► 136–139). For dinner, good music and a great atmosphere try Monastiri (► 151).

Day Four

Morning/Lunch
See Chania's market, Archaeological Museum and Folklore Museum. Arrive promptly at 1pm to get a table at Amphora (► 151).

Afternoon
Allow plenty of time to see the Byzantine Museum and the Naval Museum, and to enjoy the beautiful Venetian harbour.

Evening
Wander through the Turkish quarter to the superb Well of the Turk restaurant (► 152).

Day Five

Morning
Spend the day at the **4 Faragi Samarias** (left, ► 140–141). Take lunch and water with you.

Evening
Back in Chania, relax over a meal around the harbour, where the Tamam (► 151) is best for live music.

❶ Moni Arkadiou

Standing proudly at the end of a steep, twisting road on the edge of the Psiloreitis Mountains, the Arkadi Monastery has one of the finest Venetian churches on Crete. But its striking façade is not the only reason to visit. The tragic events that took place here in 1866 have made it a national symbol of Crete's heroic struggle for independence.

During the 1866 rebellion against the Turks, nearly 300 guerrilla fighters and some 700 women and children took refuge in the monastery. The Turks laid siege to it, and after three days broke through the gates on 9 November. As they rushed in, the abbot ordered the ignition of the gunpowder stores, killing hundreds of Cretans and Turks alike in the massive explosion: it was a heroic act of sacrifice that galvanised support for Cretan independence both at home and abroad.

Inside the church at Arkadiou

Exploring the Monastery

Standing in the centre of the courtyard is the **church**, dating from 1587, with its lovely façade of golden stone and bell tower. Inside is a beautifully carved altar screen of cypress wood, executed in 1902. On the right-hand side is a large gilt-framed icon of Christ, part of a scene of the Resurrection from the church's original altar screen.

Skulls of the martyrs in the ossuary

To the left of the church is the **refectory**, where 36 freedom fighters were massacred. You can still see sword marks on the long wooden table and benches. A room above the refectory is hung with portraits of Cretan patriots throughout history.

At the far left side of the courtyard you can step down into the roofless **gunpowder magazine** – formerly the monks' wine cellar – where the holocaust took place. A simple shrine commemorates the tragedy.

On the opposite side of the courtyard, the old **cloisters** with their arched stone arcade are very atmospheric. Above, a small **museum** houses historic items from the monastery, including a fragment of the Sacred Banner, so called because after being taken by a Turk during the Turkish onslaught the banner survived and was returned to the monastery in 1870. You can still see the battered old refectory door with bullet holes visible.

The **ossuary**, housed in a former windmill outside the gate near the parking area, contains the skulls and bones of the people who died in the great explosion.

TAKING A BREAK

With nothing else in the area, it's as well that the monastery has its own café – simple but fine for a meal or snack.

🔲 182 C4 ✉ 25km (16 miles) southeast of Rethymno ☎ 28310-72731/34; www.arkadi.org ⏰ Daily 8–7 🍴 Café (€€) 🚌 Direct buses from Rethymno 💶 Inexpensive ❓ Photography allowed, except in church and museum

---

MONI ARKADIOU: INSIDE INFO

Top tip If driving towards **Eleftherna** (➤ 142–143) note that the road is the one that appears to go through the monastery grounds. The signpost is at the far end.

Hidden gems Take a close look at the **crucifixes** high on either side of the church's altar screen. Each has a ladder propped up against the cross, and a skull and crossbones at the foot.

■ In the courtyard outside the refectory you'll find an ancient **cypress tree** with a shell from the Turkish siege still embedded in its trunk. An arrow marks the spot.

2 Rethymno

Rethymno's massive fortress – thought to be the biggest the Venetians ever built – dwarfs its tiny Venetian harbour. Nearby, the compact old quarter, punctuated with crumbling mosques and overhanging closed wooden balconies, bears traces of Turkish rule. This is Crete's third largest town, and many prefer it to its bigger neighbour, Chania. It has charm as well as modern bustle, not to mention good seafood and one of the best beaches on the northern coast.

While little remains from the ancient Minoan settlement here, you can still see plenty from the town's Greco-Roman days, when Rethymno was a busy port and trading centre. With the arrival of the Venetians in the 13th century the town positively boomed, adding a reputation for art and literature to its name. It is still considered the intellectual capital of Crete.

The fortress towers over the city from its western promontory. Below, the tiny Venetian harbour is big enough to accommodate only the smaller craft of local fishermen. Bigger ferries have to moor along the breakwater outside the narrow entrance, beside which stands a graceful 16th-century lighthouse. These days there are far more lights from the dozens of fish restaurants that ring the inner side of the harbour than from boats; waiters almost drag you inside to look at the glistening fresh fish on display.

The Town's Main Sights

From the harbour, a long palm-lined promenade – somewhat marred by the parked cars alongside – stretches east along the wide, sandy beach that runs for several miles. South of the

Rethymno boasts perhaps the biggest Venetian fortress in the world

seafront, the warren of streets that make up the old quarter lies between the fortress and Platia Iroon.

The formidable Venetian fortress, or **Fortezza**, was built in the 1570s to guard against pirates and the increasingly powerful Turks. However, it did not hold the latter out for long as they stormed the fortress in 1646 after a 23-day siege. The spacious grounds feel rather like a town park, with the remains of administrative buildings, a church and barracks. The highlight is the **mosque** with its enormous dome and tiled prayer niche. This and other buildings often house art exhibitions. You'll get spectacular views from the ramparts and parapets, but to fully appreciate the Fortezza's size walk around its base beside the rocky shoreline.

Opposite the entrance to the fortress is Rethymno's small but engaging **Archaeological Museum**. Among the highlights are neolithic finds, a collection of delicate and detailed bronze vessels from the tomb of an athlete dating from the 1st century BC, bronze figurines recovered from a shipwreck off Agia Galini, and a fine clay model of a small Minoan temple (2100–1600 BC). The artwork of bulls and other animals on the Minoan sarcophagi is also marvellous. Among the more unusual objects are a soldier's helmet made from boars' tusks,

an ivory-handled bronze mirror of the Post-Palace period (1400–1150 BC), and a small collection of red-figure vases dating from the 4th to 1st century BC on which the keen-eyed observer might spot some erotic scenes.

Near by is the **Rethymno Centre for Contemporary Art**, also known as the Kanakakis Municipal Gallery. This wonderfully restored old building has wooden rafters and white-painted Venetian arches on the ground floor. Although small, the centre has a sense of light and space, and the two floors usually house two or three changing exhibitions featuring Cretan artists. In the streets of the old town a few smaller galleries also display exhibitions.

Rethymno's other major museum is the **Historical and Folk Art Museum**, housed in an elegant early 17th-century Venetian mansion. The ground floor displays contains documents, letters and photographs on social aspects of Rethymno life while the upstairs rooms contain a fascinating collection of folk art, with detailed information panels in both Greek and English. In the large main room there are superb displays of embroidery and weaving, as well as figures wearing traditional costumes.

A smaller room is filled with ceramics and Cretan baskets, together with a potter's wheel and an interesting display on bee-keeping. The next room contains more examples of embroidery, delicate crochet and threadwork. The final room concentrates on agriculture, with scale models of a watermill, an olive press and a fulling mill – a device used for cleaning tough goatskins, traditionally made into cloaks. Picture panels on breadmaking show how the intricate decorated loaves are made for different celebrations.

Minaret of the Nerantzes Mosque

Hidden Charms

Some of Rethymno's greatest charms are found simply by wandering through the atmospheric streets of the old quarter, where you'll discover hidden fountains, decorative doorways gracing old Venetian mansions, and the overhanging wooden balconies added by the Turks.

Further along Vernardou Street from the folk museum is the **Nerantzes Mosque**, with its slender minaret soaring over the old town. It is now a music conservatory and concert hall.

Near by, at Platia Petihaki, the delightful **Rimondi Fountain** has waterspouts in the shape of the heads of the lions of St Mark. It dates from around 1626 when, it is claimed, the Venetian governor of Rethymno was envious of the Morosini Fountain in Iraklio. This small square, packed with bars and cafés, buzzes day and night.

Just back from the inner harbour, the 16th-century **loggia**

Flowers in the old town

is one of the finest examples of Renaissance architecture on Crete, once used as a gathering place for the city worthies. Today it houses the **Museum Shop** (➤ 153).

Souliou and Ethnikis Andistasis streets lead up to the **Porta Guora**, the only remnant of the old city walls. Through this archway the busy Platia Martiron, with the large modern **Church of the Four Martyrs** at one end, marks the end of the old town. Opposite are the lush **public gardens**.

TAKING A BREAK

The restaurants around the tiny harbour look appealing, but the persistent waiters can be a nuisance. **Walk further west** to a quieter row of restaurants which are just as good.

The Venetian lighthouse guards the harbour

Rethymno
🕂 182 B4

Venetian Fortress (The Fortezza)
☎ 28310-28101 🕐 Tue–Sun 10–5; last admission 4:15pm 💷 Inexpensive
❓ Photography allowed

Archaeological Museum
✉ The Fortezza ☎ 28310-55468 🕐 Tue–Sun 8:30–3 💷 Moderate ❓ No flash photography
❓ No photography allowed

Rethymno Centre for Contemporary Art
✉ Himaras 5 ☎ 28310-55530; www.rca.gr
🕐 Tue, Thu–Sun 9–2, Wed 5–9pm 💷 Moderate
❓ No photography allowed

Historical and Folk Art Museum
✉ M Vernardou 28–30 ☎ 28310-23398
🕐 Mon–Sat 9–2 💷 Moderate
❓ No photography allowed

RETHYMNO: INSIDE INFO

Top tip Parking is a nightmare and the town a warren of narrow one-way streets. On arrival, use one of the large, inexpensive **public car parks** adjacent to the ferry dock or the public gardens (buy parking cards from kiosks), then seek advice from your hotel if you are staying.

Hidden gems The city's beautiful mosques, both closed, are **Kara Musa Pasa**, at the end of Arkadiou Street near Platia Iroon, and **Veli Pasa**, with a graceful minaret and three domes, set in an overgrown garden south of the town hall at the end of Dimoukratias.

One to miss The ground floor of the Historical and Folk Art Museum could be missed. If you're in a hurry head into the garden and up to the first floor.

3 Chania

The island's second city has been called the Venice of Crete, not because of its canals (there aren't any) but because of its lovely Venetian architecture. One of the most beautiful spots on the whole island is Chania's Venetian harbour, especially at night when the lights come on and the crowds are out enjoying the many cafés and restaurants. Behind here the narrow streets of the old town are a delight to wander in, and with its wealth of museums, shopping, nightlife, town beach and good restaurants, Chania is a joy to visit.

Chania is thought to be one of the oldest continually inhabited cities in the world. There was a Minoan settlement here and modern Chania bears influences of a steady stream of invaders: Roman, Byzantine, Venetian, Genoese, Turkish and, during World War II, German.

The Venetian lighthouse at sunset

The Harbour

The greatest legacy is the Venetian harbour, actually two harbours joined together. They meet at Platia Sindrivani, or Harbour Square. Here, the **Mosque of the Janissaries** was built in 1645, the same year that the Turks took Crete from the Venetians, making it the oldest Turkish building on the island. Now renovated, it is sporadically used for staging exhibitions.

Follow Akti Tombazi east past the yachts and fishing boats moored in the inner harbour. On the right you'll pass the remains of the Venetian *arsenali*, or shipyards. You can walk all the way around the inner harbour and along the sea wall to the Venetian **lighthouse**, beautifully restored and a symbol of the city. There are lovely views back over the town and harbour.

To the west of Harbour Square the waterfront, lined with lively pavement cafés, bars and restaurants, leads to the Venetian **fortress**, or Firkas, where restoration is in progress. Inside the bastion is the **Maritime Museum of Crete**, which

The Venetian shipyards still line the harbour

Bottom: Greek flags mark the Naval Museum

is well worth visiting even if you're not that interested in naval matters. The upper floor has an extensive exhibition on the Battle of Crete (➤ 22–24). This fascinating display is poorly organised but it shows what life was like on the island at that time, particularly around Chania where much of the initial action took place. Part of the display is harrowing, especially photographs of Cretan villagers being led to their execution.

The rest of the museum includes a beautifully detailed scale model of Venetian Chania, models of ships from ancient triremes (Greek warships powered by oarsmen) to modern battleships, a room full of sea shells ranging from a metre across to the size of a pin-head, and interesting models of famous sea battles.

On the western side of the fortress is the delightful **Byzantine Museum**, whose bright modern displays are housed in a small renovated church. Whereas many Byzantine museums concentrate almost solely on icons, this one covers all aspects of Byzantine culture including sculptures, mosaics, jewellery and frescoes. There are fragments of wonderful 11th-century wall frescoes that have survived marvellously, their colours shiny and bright.

In a side gallery, the **San Salvatore collection** of Byzantine coins includes finds from graves, with lovely necklaces of glass beads, crosses, rings, domestic pottery and a 6th- to 7th-century bronze lamp with a cross in its handle. At the far end, note the icon of St George slaying the dragon. This skilful work was done by Emmanuel Tzanes Bouniales (1610–90), one of the leading lights of the Cretan School of artists (➤ 32–33).

The Old Town

To reach the town beach continue along the waterfront for about ten minutes, though Chania's better beaches are found west of town. Otherwise, turn left along Odos Theotokopoulou outside the Byzantine Museum to enter the narrow and mostly traffic-free streets of the **old town**, which lies between the harbour and the old city wall. Just wandering around here is a delight. Gift shops alternate with Venetian palaces, many now turned into some of the city's most characterful hotels. Look for ornate doorways, balconies and other remnants of Venetian splendour as you head towards the picturesque Renieri Gate.

Odos Halidhon, the major thoroughfare

running south from Harbour Square, marks the edge of the old town. Tucked back off a narrow passageway, beside the Catholic church, is the **Cretan House Folklore Museum**, a tiny, charming place with tableaux of weavers, basketmakers and other artisans. The two founders of the museum have a workshop here where their own weavings and embroideries are for sale.

A Roman mosaic in the Archaeological Museum

Near by, Chania's splendid **Archaeological Museum** is atmospherically housed beneath the arched roof of the restored Venetian Church of San Francesco. You'll find plenty of information in both Greek and English as you tour the exhibits in clockwise fashion. Case 10 holds one of the most interesting exhibits: rare seals with Minoan Linear A script, accidentally preserved in a fire, are shown alongside examples of Linear B. Kastelli Chania is the only place outside Knossos where both Linear A and B have been found. Though Linear A remains a mystery, here some symbols have been deciphered. Pictographs for such things as sheep, ox, wine, olive oil, figs and numerals – a simple circle represents 100 – indicate an advanced system of accounting.

The museum has many other fine objects, including toys belonging to Minoan children, which were used as burial offerings, and magnificent Roman floor mosaics from Chania houses. In a small annexe, the Mitsotakis Collection comprises Minoan and Mycenaean items, vases, pots, figurines, early Iron Age vases and bowls, Minoan metalwork and many other fine items. At the far end of the gallery a central case contains the only known bronze vessel to be embossed with a Linear A inscription, found at the peak sanctuary at Kofinas. It was originally made in Egypt around 1800–1425 BC, then brought to Crete and engraved on the island.

Carpets are still handwoven in Chania

Beyond the Old Town

From the museum, Odos Halidhon leads south past the rather nondescript cathedral to modern Chania. Turn left on Odos Skridlof to reach the bustling **covered market**, with butchers, honey and cheese vendors, fruit and vegetable stalls and other shops lining the cross-shaped aisles.

Between the market and the inner harbour, the **Spiantza quarter** is one of the most atmospheric places in Chania. As you wander around the residential streets of this former Turkish area, you'll find cobbled streets, charming old houses with wooden balconies and archways, and minarets peeking out above the rooftops.

TAKING A BREAK

Anywhere on the **Venetian harbour** has a great setting and atmosphere, but if you care about your food try the **Amphora** (➤ 151).

Chania
✚ 181 E4

Maritime Museum of Crete
✉ Akti Koundourioti ☎ 28210-91875 ⏱ Daily 9–4 (9–2 in winter)
🎫 Moderate ❓ No flash photography

Byzantine Museum
✉ The Fortress ⏱ Tue–Sun 8:30–3 🎫 Free ❓ No photography

Cretan House Folklore Museum
✉ Odos Halidhon 46B ☎ 28210-52606 ⏱ Apr–Oct Sun–Fri 9–2 🎫 Free
❓ Photography allowed

A hint of old Venice in Chania's harbour

Archaeological Museum
✉ Odos Halidhon 21 ☎ 28210-90334 ⏱ Tue–Sun 8:30–3 🎫 Inexpensive
❓ No flash photography

CHANIA: INSIDE INFO

Top tip If driving into Chania, there is **good parking** just to the west of the fortress, allowing easy access to the old town and most of the city's attractions.

Hidden gems The **Etz Hayyim Synagogue** off Odos Kondylaki is still in use but can be visited for its small historical displays and lovely peaceful garden.
■ In the Kastelli quarter behind the inner harbour archaeological digs are uncovering the remains of **Minoan Kydonia**. Sites can be seen along or just off Odos Kanevaro.

4 Faragi Samarias

The scenery of the Samaria Gorge makes it Crete's most spectacular natural wonder. This is the longest gorge in Europe, stretching 18km (11 miles) from the Omalos Plateau, 1,100m (3,610 feet) high in the Lefka Ori (White Mountains), to the Libyan Sea. The trek from top to bottom is long, hot and tiring, rather than difficult, but do it if you're reasonably fit – it's an experience you'll never forget.

The Faragi Samarias became a national park in 1962. It shelters a fascinating array of plants and wildlife, including ancient pine and cypress, wild orchids and dittany, and endangered species such as the golden eagle and the Cretan ibex, or krí-krí (➤ 30). This dramatic ravine was formed by a river, which slows to a trickle in summer but becomes a raging torrent after winter snow and rains. Thus the gorge is only open from May to October, weather permitting.

Thousands of people hike the gorge every year, and in high season it can seem an endless procession. Do use common sense before undertaking the trek and make sure you (and your young children) are up to the entire 16km (10 mile) walk, which takes 5 to 7 hours – there are no short-cuts out of the gorge once you start. It requires stamina, especially in the heat, and although it is downhill all the way knees and ankles will soon feel the strain.

Take a hat, sunglasses and sun block, as there is no shade for the last few kilometres, and bring at least a litre of water per person – there are places to top up with spring water along the way. Above all, wear appropriate shoes with good support and strong soles to withstand sharp rocks. If you follow those simple guidelines, you'll enjoy the walk and feel a great sense of achievement at the end.

The easiest way to walk the Faragi Samarias is with an organised tour; transport details are sorted out for you, and a guide will accompany your group. But you can also take an early bus from Chania to the top of the gorge. From Agia Roumeli at the lower end you catch a ferry to Chora Sfakion to connect with a return bus. Check all times locally.

SAMARIA THE LAZY WAY

Tour companies offer an easier option. A ferry takes you to Agia Roumeli, where you can walk up the gorge to the dramatic Sideroportes.

Hiking the Gorge

The *xilóskalo* (wooden staircase), cut from the rock, makes a steep, winding descent into the gorge. The mountain views are breathtaking, with the sheer rock face of Mount Gingilos (2,080m/6,825 feet) towering magnificently above through the pines. The path becomes flatter after about 4km (2.5 miles), at the stone chapel of **Agios Nikolaos**. Baby *krí-krí*

Looking up to Mount Gingilos at the entrance to Samaria

sometimes venture down to graze at this shady spot beside the river.

Climb over the dry boulders and continue on to the abandoned village of **Samaria**, whose residents were relocated when the park was formed. The Church of Ossia Maria (Mary's Bones) dates from the early 14th century. This is nearly the halfway point, and a good picnic spot. You will find a warden's station here.

Beyond, the gorge deepens beneath dramatic cliffs and you criss-cross the stream several times on the approach to the **Sideroportes** (Iron Gates). These sheer rock walls rise up over 300m (984 feet) high but are only 3.5m (11 feet) wide, the narrowest point in the gorge. Beyond, the path abruptly opens out to a flat, shadeless riverbed. At the end of the park it's a further gruelling 2km (1 mile) in the hot sun to **Agia Roumeli**, whose tavernas are a welcome sight.

TAKING A BREAK

Bring a **picnic** as there are no refreshments until you reach the end of the gorge.

➕ 181 D2 🚌 Bus from Chania for Omalos/Samaria

FARAGI SAMARIAS: INSIDE INFO

Top tips Don't be fooled by the kilometre markers; they only mark distances within the park, not the full length of the walk.

■ **Park wardens** patrol the gorge to make sure no one is left overnight, and mules stand by to rescue the injured.

■ Get an **early start**. You'll have more time to linger without worrying about missing the boat.

■ If your **footwear is inadequate** you may not be allowed to enter the gorge

■ Note that this walk is not possible in winter.

At Your Leisure

5 Spilaio Melidoniou

Whereas other caves on Crete are filled with myths and legends, the Melidoniou Cave is filled with the spirits of the people who died there, and it is one of the most chilling memorials on the island. In 1824, while the Cretans were fighting for their independence from the Turks, 300 villagers hid inside the cave from approaching Turkish forces. When asked to surrender the villagers refused, at which point the Turkish commander blocked the cave entrance to stop the air supply. The villagers created new air holes in the network of passages but the Turks were equally quick to seal these. They then opened the cave entrance slightly and lit fires at the mouth so smoked poured in and everyone inside choked to death. A memorial in the centre of the cave marks the spot where the bones of the people were gathered together years later and buried.

Without this background the cave would merely be an interesting natural phenomenon, comprising one large chamber at the foot of a staircase carved out of the rocks. This can be slippery and is also very

poorly lit, so take a torch if you can. New areas of the cave are still being explored, and though shown on the map in the official booklet they may not be open.

🔢 183 D4 ✉ Near Melidoni 🕐 Apr–Oct daily 9–6:30/7pm 🚌 Bus to Perama from Rethymno 💰 Moderate ❓ Photography allowed

6 Margarites

There can be no better place on the island to buy ceramics than in the hill village of Margarites, where pottery is a tradition and many artisans have their workshops. As the main road winds through the village, bright displays of pottery can be seen on every corner. Several of the craftsmen produce similar goods (bowls, jugs, plates, vases) distinguished only by their patterns and colours, but a few produce work of a very distinctive style and to a very high standard, so take the time to explore the different workshops. Even if you don't plan to buy, the pretty town is a delightful place to wander around.

🔢 182 C4 🚌 Bus from Rethymno

7 Eleftherna

The site of the city of Archea Eleftherna (Ancient Eleftherna) is one of the most impressive on the island, set in a valley high in the hills

At work in the potters' village of Margarites

Spili is a good place to break a journey

between two villages. Don't stop in the village of Eleftherna itself (you can reach the site from there but it is a long walk) but go on to Archea Eleftherna from where the remains are more easily reached. Like Lato (► 104–105), Eleftherna was a major Doric city and later a Roman settlement before falling into ruin. Not too many remains can be seen today, but the setting is superb.

✚ 182 C4 ✉ Archea Eleftherna ⊙ Open access 🚌 Bus from Rethymno 💶 Free ❓ Photography allowed

🛭 North Coast Beaches

The beaches along the north coast in this part of the island include long stretches of golden sand, with several busy holiday spots among them. West of Iraklio the first two main resorts are **Bali** (✚ 183 D4) and **Panormos** (✚ 182 C4), the latter being the smaller but with the better beach. It is only west of here, though, that the beaches come into their own. East of Rethymno, and in the town itself, are some lovely stretches of sand, with more to be found if you carry on driving west towards Chania. Look for the sign for **Petres Bridge**, where there is access to a beautiful long beach with a few cafés, sunbeds and parasols. Parking and

more facilities can be found opposite the turning for Episkopi, with golden sand running for miles.

One of the most attractive resorts is **Georgioupoli** (✚ 181 F3), with a wide sandy beach backed by dunes. The town itself has not lost its character despite being popular with visitors. **Kalives** (✚ 181 F4), closer to Chania, also has a good sandy beach. **Platanias** (✚ 171 D4) is a large, lively resort west of Chania with a booming nightlife scene in summer.

🛭 Spili

One of the main towns between Rethymno and the south coast, Spili is the ideal place to break a journey. Huddled beneath mountain slopes, its back streets are those of a busy hill town, a world away from the holiday resorts on the coast. In the centre of the town on a small square a delightful Venetian fountain comprises a row of 19 lions' heads spouting water into a stone trough. There are a number of atmospheric tavernas that make a wonderful lunch stop.

✚ 182 B3 🚌 Bus from Rethymno

⑩ Moni Preveli

The monastery at Preveli is one of the loveliest in the whole of southern Crete and has a revered place in Greek history for its role in the Battle of Crete (► 22–25). During World War II the monks here risked the wrath (and worse) of the Nazis by providing shelter to Allied troops trapped on Crete after the evacuation, and subsequently aided the Cretan resistance movement.

Originally dating back to the 17th century, the monastery's isolated setting and grounds dotted with palm trees and pomegranate trees are irresistible to the photographer. Within the "lion-coloured" walled enclosure is a chapel, the cells where the monks still live and peaceful courtyards.

One of the monastery's cellars has been effectively turned into a small museum, a long and narrow vaulted room whose alcoves and cabinets contain icons, vestments,

The monastery at Preveli

bibles and other religious items. The magnificently adorned chapel has an elaborate gold and red Bishop's Chair, an ornate pulpit, icon-covered walls and, in the centre, a cross said to contain a piece of the True Cross.

In the courtyard near by an old fountain exhorts visitors to wash their faces and wash their sins away. For those who want to bathe more fully, there are several good beaches close by, including **Preveli Beach** and **Palm Beach**, both accessible by following the main road eastward from the monastery.

➕ 182 B3 ☎ 28320-312461; www.preveli. org ⚙ 25 Mar–31 May Daily 8–7; 1 Jun–31 Oct Mon–Sat 8–1, 3–7, Sun 8–7 🚌 Buses from Rethymno and to/from Plakias 💷 Inexpensive ❓ Photography allowed except in church and museum

⑪ Plakias

With its long, wide beach backed by tamarisk trees, Plakias is a terrific south coast retreat for those who want to get away from it all without completely leaving civilisation behind. There are a few hotels, bars and tavernas, and although the resort bears little resemblance to what it was 20 years ago, it's still attractive, with a long promenade, a more remote feel than many other resorts on Crete and plenty to do. A long curve of sand sweeps away at the eastern end of town, and you'll find more good beaches if you continue along the coast to the west. You can take hill walks to the north or walk to the monastery at Preveli (➤ 144), while drivers can enjoy two of Crete's most dramatic gorges, **Kotsifou** and **Kourtaliotiko**, to the north.

🗺 182 A3 🚌 Buses from Rethymno and Agia Galini

🔢 Frangokastello

The Venetian fortress at Frangokastello is one of the largest

DEW IN THE MORNING

In May 1828 the Greeks raised their flag at the fortress in defiance of the ruling Turks and in the subsequent battle 385 Cretans were killed. Locals claim that every year, on 28 May, these souls can be seen marching towards Frangokastello. The dead are called *droussoulites*, or dew shades, because they are said to appear with the morning dew.

on the island. Built in this remote setting in 1371 to help protect the south coast from pirates and other raiders, it was also used to keep unruly locals in check. However, the fortress's imposing nature is somewhat undermined when you discover that today it is a mere shell, with nothing inside the sturdy walls. Still, it stands on a lovely spot with good beaches and marshland where wildlife flourishes close by.

🗺 181 F2 🕐 Open access 🍴 Several beach tavernas, including Flisbos and Korali (€–€€) 🚌 Plakias– Chora Sfakion buses pass by

🔢 Faragi Imbrou

Samaria (➤ 140–141) may be more famous and more dramatic, but the Faragi Imbrou (Impros Gorge) offers a good half-day's walk through some of southern Crete's most spectacular scenery. It is also more accessible and not as crammed with other walkers. The entrance is just south of the village of Impros and the gorge runs for about 6km (4 miles) towards the sea, stopping just short of the coast. It can be tackled easily by anyone who is reasonably fit, and the rock formations, deep sides and abundant wild flowers in spring are superb. Tour companies in nearby towns offer organised trips, which are worth considering, as a one-way walk – even if you have your own car – needs a little organising.

🗺 181 F2 🕐 Open access 🍴 Café serving light meals at start and end of walk (€) 🚌 Buses to Impros village from Chania and Chora Sfakion

Looking down the Impros Gorge

14 Chora Sfakion

The main town of southern Crete's Sfakia region has an atmosphere all its own. Its lazy charm and lovely coastal setting, together with the peace that descends when the day's visitors have left, will captivate anyone who spends a few days here. The focus of the town is its small harbour, lined on one side with cafés and restaurants. Beyond here the streets start to rise, some steeply, hemmed in as the town is by the lower slopes of the Levka Ori, or White Mountains. It was through these mountains that Allied troops were evacuated after the Battle of

Pleasant waterside restaurants overlook the harbour at Chora Sfakion

Crete (➤ 22–25), arriving exhausted at Chora Sfakion to await the rescuing ships. Today there is only a small pebble beach, but there are better beaches along the nearby coasts, good walks in the mountains and a get-away-from-it-all feeling.

🕇 181 E2 🍴 Numerous cafés and tavernas line the harbour (€–€€) 🚌 Bus from Chania

15 Gavdos Island

The largest of Crete's offshore islands, Gavdos is also the most southerly point in Europe. It takes a bit of a hike to get to the island's southern tip, but a visit here will show you a part of Crete that few people see. With a resident population of about 50, facilities are few, but you might find a room to rent and many people camp here in the summer. One or two small cafés serve simple food in summer and beaches are good, if you don't mind a walk to get to them. However, while Gavdos might seem like heaven, it is not for everyone.

🚩 181 E1 (inset) 🍴 Some cafés (€)
⛴ Summer ferries from Chora Sfakion and Palaiochora

🔟 Loutro

Loutro, with its blue and white buildings set around a cove against a stunning mountain backdrop, is one of the most picturesque villages on the island. There is nothing to do here – the tiny village is little more than a waterfront strip with several tavernas and rooms to rent – but that is where the attraction lies for many visitors. You needn't waste time looking for the road to Loutro, as there isn't one: you either need to walk from the nearest road a few kilometres away, or do what most people do and take the boat in and out. If you tire of the small pebble beach there are good coastal walks in both directions

FOR CHILDREN

The **Fortezza** at Rethymno (► 133)
The **Little Trains** in Chania and Rethymno
Horse and buggy ride in Chania
Spilaio Melidoniou (► 142)
The **beach** and **castle** at Frangokastello (► 145)
Beaches everywhere

to better beaches, or you can head inland to the mountains. Despite the influx of visitors in summer, vastly outnumbering local people, in comparison to most places on Crete Loutro remains an idyllic retreat.

🚩 181 E2 🍴 Several simple cafés (€–€€)
⛴ Boats from Chora Sfakion and other south coast towns

Allied graves at Souda

🔟 Souda and Akrotiri

The Akrotiri Peninsula, to the immediate east of Chania, is often neglected by visitors but it offers lovely hill scenery, ancient monasteries and some of the most peaceful spots on the north coast – despite the fact that Chania's airport and ferry port are both located here.

No roads lead to Loutro

The growing resort of Palaiochora

The easiest way of getting to the peninsula from Chania is to drive east out of the town centre towards the airport and follow the occasional signs for the Venizélos Graves. These are on a hillside in a small garden, with terrific views over the city. Crete's premier politician and one-time Greek leader, Elefthérios Venizélos, lies buried here, and close by is the grave of his son, Sophocles.

Further out on the peninsula are three monasteries – **Agia Triada, Gouvernetou** and **Korakies**. Agia Triada, with its orange-coloured walls, is particularly beautiful and should not be missed. The others are a few kilometres beyond up a winding road.

Souda, on the bay of the same name, is on the far side of the peninsula. On the outskirts of the town is the beautiful and peaceful **Allied War Cemetery**, where lie hundreds of soldiers who died during World War II. The headstones look out over the water, the young men buried in the soil of the island they tried to defend.

✚ 181 E4 **Allied War Cemetery** ✉ 1km (0.5 miles) northwest of Souda 🕐 Open access 🍴 Plenty of cafés and restaurants in Souda (€) 💰 Free ❓ Photography allowed

🔢 Palaiochora

The major resort in southwest Crete is Palaiochora, an appealing town with two beaches either side of a headland and a great deal of easy-going charm. Standing on the headland are the ruins of a Venetian fortress dating back to 1279, with a sandy beach to the west and a pebble beach to the east. The south coast can be quite windy, and they do say that if one beach is affected by the wind the other one will be sheltered, but that isn't always the case.

The town has developed rapidly as a tourist resort over the last ten years or so, and many hotels, rooms to rent, souvenir shops, travel agents and restaurants have sprung up. Despite that, its identity as a town has not been lost, especially on the main street at night when traffic is banned, chairs spill out from cafés and bars, the air is filled with the chatter of conversation and people enjoy wandering round in a very relaxed atmosphere.

✚ 180 B2 🍴 Numerous cafés and restaurants (€–€€€) 🚌 Bus from Chania

Where to... Stay

Prices

Prices are for a double room per night in high season including taxes

€ under €70 €€ €70–€150 €€€ over €150

CHANIA

Casa Delfino €€€

The best place in town is this 17th-century former palace, built around a fabulous Venetian-style courtyard. All the studio rooms, ordinary rooms and suites are bright and cheerful and superbly decorated with old photos on the walls. Air-conditioning (with individual controls), mini-bar, satellite TVs, DVD players and marble Jacuzzi baths are standard, as is high-speed internet access in the rooms There's a large bar, a breakfast room, a roof terrace and a lounge, tucked away in the old quarter.

➕ 181 E4 ✉ Theofanous 9, Chania
☎ 28210-87400/93098;
www.casadelfino.com

Hotel El Greco €€

Perfectly situated on an almost traffic-free street in the old town, just a minute's walk from the harbour, the El Greco is a family-run hotel with only 23 rooms. They are all a good size and well appointed, some being suites with extra living space. They all have air-conditioning, TVs, phones and the welcome bonus of a fridge. There's a relaxing bar downstairs and a terrific roof garden with wonderful views over the roofs of the old town to the sea.

➕ 181 E4 ✉ Theotokopoulos 49, Chania
☎ 28210-94030/90432/9118;
www.grecotel.gr ⊙ Mar–Nov

Ifigenia Rooms and Studios €€

Not one hotel but several places close together near the Venetian harbour, all are owned by the same enterprising young man and all have the same flair when it comes to the decoration. Some of the rooms are stunningly designed with stone arches, four-poster beds, galleried areas and open-plan baths adding to the striking look. As well as the Ifigenia I, II and III there are the Ifigenia Studios, Pension Orio and Hotel Captain Vassilis.

➕ 181 E4 ✉ Angelou 18 and others, Chania
☎ 28210-99184 or 0944-501319 (mobile);
www.ifigeniastudios.gr

Palazzo Hotel €€

You'll find this delightful small hotel on a quiet street in the old town. It was once a mansion and the rooms,

named after Greek gods and heroes, are full of wood-panelling and old-fashioned touches, though with modern bathrooms, TVs, fridges and phones. The generous breakfast is one reason to stay here, others being the friendly service and ideal location: use the public car park west of the harbour if you are driving.

➕ 181 E4 ✉ Theotokopoulou 54, Chania
☎ 28210-93227; www.palazzodipietro.com
⊙ Mar–Nov

CHORA SKAFION

Vritomartis Hotel and Bungalows €€

One of the best and best-run hotels on Crete, the Vritomartis has its own pool and restaurant, and grounds lush with vegetation. It is also Greece's only naturist hotel, though non-naturists are also welcome and nudity is not allowed inside the hotel buildings. The rooms are big, bright and white, and all have balconies though` some only overlook the car park. There is also a large bar and a restaurant, and organised activities and tours.

⊞ 181 E2 ⊠ Chora Sfakion
☎ 28250-91112; www.naturism-crete.com
⊙ Apr–Oct

Galaxy Rooms €

Galaxy is one of the most pleasant of the many "rooms to rent" options in Palaiochora. The front rooms, above the Galaxy Fish Restaurant, have large balconies overlooking the town's pebble beach and the sea. The ensuite rooms are a good size and surprisingly well equipped with TV, fridge, phone and washing line. They are also clean and well maintained. Though no breakfast is served on site, there are several choices near by. The owner also has more rooms across town near the sandy beach.

⊞ 180 B2 ⊠ Palaiochora
☎ 28230-41059/41514;⊙ Apr–Oct

Hotel Fortezza €€

This modern hotel is in one of the quieter areas of Rethymno, mostly pedestrianised and close to the Venetian fort that gives the hotel its name. It's also not far from the beach. The best rooms have balconies and overlook the small swimming pool, so try to get one of these. Booking is recommended, even in low season.

⊞ 181 B4 ⊠ Melisinou 16, Rethymno
☎ 28310-23828/55551; www.fortezza.gr

Grecotel Creta Palace €€

Although a deluxe hotel, prices are reasonable given its quality and location; it's about 4km (2.5 miles) east of Rethymno centre, beyond the wonderful town beach. The rooms are elegant, bright and clean, and the hotel has all the facilities you might expect including three swimming pools (one indoors), restaurants, bars, gym, tennis courts and water sports.

⊞ 182 B4 ⊠ Misiria Beach, Rethymno
☎ 28310-55181; www.grecotel.gr
⊙ Apr–Oct

Hotel Ideon €€

In a wonderful location overlooking the harbour, the Ideon is set back from the main road and has a public car park (vital in Rethymno) directly opposite. The hotel has 100 rooms, all with balconies overlooking either the sea or the private swimming pool. The rooms are modern, with phone, radio, safe, air-conditioning and bath. The slightly pricier suites also have a fridge and TV.

⊞ 182 B4 ⊠ Platia Plastira 10, Rethymno
☎ 28310-28667; www.hotelideon.gr
⊙ Mar–Oct

Palazzo Rimondi €€€

Tucked away in the back streets of the old town, the Rimondi is a small, stylish hotel that spreads over several 15th-century Venetian houses. The conversion has been very tastefully done, retaining such features as the decorated ceilings,

while giving the rooms every modern convenience. The 21 rooms are more like mini-suites, with separate living and kitchen areas, and there's a small swimming pool in the inner courtyard.

⊞ 182 B4 ⊠ Xanthoudidou 21, Rethymno
☎ 28310-51289; www.palazzorimondi.com

Veneto €€

It's easy to understand why Veneto is popular with wedding parties. Enchantingly set in a historic stone building in the heart of the atmospheric old town, these exclusive suites make for a magical stay. The attention to detail is exquisite, from the pebble floor mosaic in the covered ground floor courtyard to the charming fountains and water features. The individually decorated rooms are traditionally furnished with lovely touches such as framed pieces of embroidery and handmade lace curtains. The in-house restaurant is excellent.

⊞ 182 B4 ⊠ Odos Epimenidou 4, Rethymno
☎ 28310 56634; www.veneto.gr

Where to...
Eat and Drink

Prices
Prices are for a two-course meal for one person, excluding drinks and tips

€ under €20   €€ €20–€40   €€€ over €40

CHANIA

Amphora €€
The food here is excellent. Fresh fish naturally features but *meze* are a speciality here, and the mixed Greek plate can certainly be recommended. The fact that they use only virgin olive oil to prepare their dishes certainly shows in the results.

☩ 181 E4 ⊠ Akti Koundouriotou 49, Chania ☎ 28210-93224 ⓒ Apr–Oct daily 11:30am–midnight

Apostolis €€
This family-owned seafood taverna at the far eastern end of the Old Harbour is one of Chania's best. The attention to detail and generosity impresses, from the half loaf of hot fresh bread and virgin olive oil that arrives after you sit down to the complimentary dessert of tasty preserved fruit, yoghurt, cheese pastries, and ouzo. Seafood-lovers should plan for a long, leisurely lunch and order the enormous, excellent-value seafood platter. If you arrive at noon you'll likely be eating alone; locals fill the place after 2pm.

☩ 181 E4 ⊠ Akti Enoseos, Chani ☎ 28210-41767 ⓒ Lunch until late

Monastiri €
Subtitled "the Hellenic Taste", this outstanding taverna serves tasty home-style Greek food and Cretan specialities with intriguing names like "The Nun's Mistake", a dish of succulent pork chops, and "The Little Devil", a long spicy village sausage. Worth trying are the wild greens, fennel pie (actually flat bread) and the melt-in-your-mouth lamb in oil and wine. Situated on the Old Harbour east of the mosque, by day you'll get views of the lighthouse but at night there's live music.

☩ 181 E4 ⊠ Akti Tompazi 12, Chania ☎ 28210-55527; www.monastiri-taverna.gr ⓒ Daily, all day

Tamam €€
Some of the best food in town can be sampled at the former Turkish bathhouse, hence the nightly queues for a table by both locals and visitors alike. Despite the passing crowds, most people prefer to sit outside in the narrow street to enjoy the imaginative dishes combining the best of the Mediterranean, from Italian risotto via Greek baked red peppers to Middle Eastern lamb with rice and yoghurt. There's a good range for vegetarians, too. The wine list includes many wines from the mainland as well as from Crete itself.

☩ 181 E4 ⊠ Zambeliou 49, Chania ☎ 28210-96080 ⓒ Daily 1pm–12:30am

Well of the Turk €€
Allow plenty of time to find this back-alley place, near Platia 1821. The search will be rewarded as British owner Jenny Payavla, who lived in Tangier, combines the best of Cretan and North African cuisine. Dishes range from shish kebabs and cous-cous to specialities including *calamari* (squid) stuffed with seafood, herbs and rice and served with turmeric rice. There's a bar inside. Don't forget to ask to see the actual Well of the Turk.

☩ 181 E4 ⊠ Kalinikou Sarpaki 1–3, Chania ☎ 28210-54547 ⓒ Wed–Mon pm–late

PALAIOCHORA

Galaxy Fish Restaurant €€

This excellent fish restaurant has roadside seating opposite the pebble beach, an upper open patio beneath a red-tiled roof and a further raised indoor seating area. Stretched across the back wall of the latter is a large fisherman's net hung with crab shells, lobsters, starfish and other sea creatures. Although there are meat options on the menu, and old Greek favourites, the speciality is quite simple, as the menu states: "fresh fish from Palaiochora". Enjoy the wine from the barrel, too.

⊞ 180 B2 ⊠ Palaiochora
☎ 28230-41059/41514 ◷ Apr–Oct daily lunch and dinner

RETHYMNO

Avli €€€

The best spot to choose here is the lovely open-roofed garden courtyard planted with large palms, though there are also tables on the street outside and in another indoor area. The menu advertises "Gastronomic experiments with Cretan produce and an open mind", and to find out if they succeed try one of the house specialities such as wild kid goat cooked with honey and thyme.

⊞ 182 B4 ⊠ Xanthoudidou 22/
Radamanthyos, Rethymno ☎ 28310-26213
◷ Daily noon–2:30, 6–midnight

Cavo d'Oro €€€

There are numerous fish restaurants cheek-by-jowl around the little Venetian harbour in Rethymno, and with every waiter trying to persuade you to eat in their establishment it can be very hard to choose between them. It is worth making the effort to find the Cavo d'Oro, which looks like all the rest with its displays of fresh fish and seafood, but is rated the best by the local people.

⊞ 182 B4 ⊠ Nearchou 42–43, Rethymno
☎ 28310-24446 ◷ Daily 11am–midnight

Makam €

This Old Town taverna is must for music-lovers. Situated in a cavernous stone building with high ceilings and rickety wooden tables and old musical instruments on the walls. There's a nightly performance of some kind, from a traditional Cretan folk trio to a classical four-piece outfit or experimental jazz group. While some come just to listen to the music, most order dishes of mezedes (servings are generous here) and settle in for the night.

⊞ 182 B4 ⊠ Nik Foka & Odos Vernardou,
Rethymno ☎ 69389-93779 ◷ Nightly, from 9pm until late

Myrogdies €

Named "Pomegranates" after the tree in the courtyard, this taverna makes good use of the tangy ingredient on its menu. The red lola salad of lettuce greens, smoked pork, goat's cheese, balsamic vinegar and pomegranate seeds is scrumptious. The young owner-chef Nikos Nektarios is helped out in the kitchen by some authentic Greek grandmothers, which explains how the kitchen manages to produce both hearty traditional dishes (the mother-in-law's sausages are delicious) and lighter Mediterranean cuisine. The live musicians are as enjoyable as the food.

⊞ 182 B4 ⊠ Odos E. Vernadou 32,
Rethymno ☎ 69726-95170 ◷ Nightly

Ousies: Meze & Spirits €

In an old stone building with wooden tables and chairs and a cosy fireplace, this casual local favourite is an atmospheric ouzeri. Order three or four mezedes per person – you can order more later – and take your time savouring Cretan specialities such as gruyere sausages fried with raki and tomatoes, and buyurdi – a casserole of layered feta and fresh tomatoes. Try to arrive by 10pm so you get table before the locals start to come in and the place starts buzzing.

⊞ 182 B4 ⊠ Odos E. Vernadou 20,
Rethymno ☎ 28310-56643 ◷ Nightly

Where to... Shop

The best shopping in western Crete is in Rethymno and Chania. For ceramics, visit the pottery village of Margarites (▶ 142). Two potters worth seeking out for quality wares are Manolis Kallergis (tel: 28340-92262) and Nikos Kavgalakis at the southern end of the village.

CHANIA

Most of the old town south of the fortress is given over to tourist shops. On Theotokopoulou, the main street, two gift shops stand out: Paraoro (No 16), selling beautiful handmade glass, ceramics and metal sculpture; and 1885 (opposite at No 11), selling handmade silver and clothes.

Roka Carpets, 61 Zambeliou, is stacked with colourful rugs,

blankets and wall hangings, all handwoven on a loom here in the shop. At Top Hanas, 3 Angelou, by the Naval Museum, old Cretan blankets and rugs are displayed in an old house. For beautiful embroidery and tablecloths made on a loom, try Pili, 40 Kriari Street, below the tourist office.

Meli, 45 Odos Kondilaki, is one of the best shops on the island for Cretan natural products. You can buy vinegar, olive oil, *raki* and wine in beautiful decorative glass bottles, honey and organic olives. At the covered market (▶ 139). shop for Cretan cheeses, herbs, spices and other foodie gifts.

Nearby Odos Skridlof is the place for leatherware, and though the old workshops are mostly gone you'll find some of the best prices for belts, bags, sandals and other

goods, even Cretan high boots. Odos Sifaka is the street of the knife-makers.

The Local Artistic Handicrafts' Association, at the old harbour behind the mosque, carries a range, in both price and quality, of ceramics, sculpture, glass and jewellery, including some very artistic pieces. Verekinthos Craft Village, just outside town at Chania Industrial Park, on the south side of the National Highway, is another good place for traditional handicrafts.

RETHYMNO

You could think of Rethymno's warren of streets as one giant bazaar. Souvenir shops abound and there is a good selection of clothing since this is the main shopping area for locals too, particularly along Odos Arkadiou. There are also many jewellery shops around town. The loggia now houses the Museum Shop for the Ministry of Culture

(open 8–3:30), where you can buy reproductions of ancient art from major museums. For antiques, try Palaiopoleiou, Souliou 40. Artistic woodturner Nikos Siragas, at Petalioti 2, creates beautiful bowls, vases and sculptures from olive and carob wood. Also try Olive Tree Wood, Arambatzoglou 35, for wooden crafts.

Manolis Stagakis and his son Michalis are two of the last *lyra* makers who carve instruments by hand. Their workshop is at Dimakopoulou 6 where you can order your own custom-made *lyra*. Ethnikis Andistasis is the market street near Porta Guora, with delicious foodstuffs. There is also a Thursday market on Dhimitrakaki, by the public gardens.

Among those bookshops carrying English titles are International Press, at Venizelou, and I Petihaki, near the waterfront. English books are expensive, but you may find a bargain at one of the second-hand bookshops around town.

Where to...
Be Entertained

RETHYMNO NIGHTLIFE

Most of the big discos can be found east of town among the large hotels. In the centre try the **Opera Club** on Salaminos, **Rock Café Fortezza** by the inner harbour and, around the corner, **NYC-Metropolis**. A number of rock bars are clustered around Platia Petihaki and the streets behind the inner harbour. **Odysseas**, on Venizelou, has nightly live Cretan music and dancing geared for tourists.

CHANIA NIGHTLIFE

Chania's largest discos are also out of town, mainly west along the coast at Platanias. **Splendid**, **Privilege** and **Mylos Club** are always packed.

In town, the main clubs are along the inner harbour, behind the mosque. These include **Club Xania** and **Klik Dancing Bar**, with **Platia** upstairs offering live Greek music. Further along the inner harbour are **Four Seasons** and **Prime Vision Ariadne**, the latter a popular venue for live modern Greek music. Chania's largest discos are **Energy**, at Halidhon, and **Skalidhi**, near the Schiavo Bastion.

MUSIC AND FESTIVALS

For traditional and contemporary Greek music in **Chania**, look for handbills advertising Cretan musicians. They often play at **Lyrakia**, a bar by the waterfront, and **Café Kriti**, behind the *arsendi*

at 22 Kalergon. Chania's cultural calendar of performances runs from mid-July to September; enquire at the tourist office (▶ 37).

The main cultural event in **Rethymno** is the **Renaissance Festival**, with international theatre and music performances held in August and September in the Venetian fortress. The programme is announced in mid-July; contact the town hall (tel: 28310-53583) for information and tickets. There is also a **Wine Festival** held in the Municipal Park in July.

BOAT TRIPS AND WATER SPORTS

Dolphin Cruises in Rethymno (tel: 28310-57666) run boat trips to pirate caves and beaches on the north coast; or cruise to Bali on a pirate ship with **Captain Hook** (tel: 28310-57666).

Boat trips are offered all along Chania's old harbour. These include a half-day cruise on **Aphrodite** (tel: 6930-2977292). Alternatively, take a trip on a glass-bottom boat with **Evagelos** (tel: 6945 874283) or the **Posidon Sea Discoverer** (tel: 28210-55838).

Limnoupolis Waterpark (tel: 28210-33246, open May–Oct 10–6:30), is 7km (4 miles) from Chania on the Omalos road.

Two dive centres in Rethymno are **Paradise Dive Centre**, 73 and 75 El Venizelou (tel: 28310-26317) and **Dolphin Diving Centre**, Hotel Rethymno mare-Scaleta (tel: 28310-71703). In Chania, try **Blue Adventurers Diving**, 69 Daskalogianni Street (tel: 28210-40608).

OTHER ACTIVITIES

In Rethymno, **Olympic Bike Travel** (tel: 28310-72383; www. olympicbike.com) offers organised bike rides in the countryside and mountain biking. **The Happy Walker**, 56 Tompazi Street (tel: 28310-52920; www.happywalker. nl), organises guided walks in the countryside from one to ten days.

Walks & Drives

1 ZAROS & FARAGI ROUVAS

Walk

This exhilarating walk takes you to a mountain monastery and up the rocky Rouvas Gorge, rich in flora and fauna, with beautiful views of central Crete's Psiloritis range. Start early to avoid the worst of the midday heat.

DISTANCE 8km (5 miles). Note that this route is impassable in winter.
TIME 3–4 hours
START/END POINT Zaros ✚ 183 E3

1–2
Zaros, nestling at the southern foot of Oros Ida (Psiloritis), is famous throughout Crete for its spring water, bottled on the edge of town. Drive west through town and park on the main road near the post office. (To shorten the walk, drive to the lake.)

2–3
Continue along the main road until you see signs for the Idi Hotel and Lake Votomos just past a modern fountain. Turn right and follow the narrow road up the hill to the **Idi Hotel** (▶ 92), about 1km (0.5 miles) from town.

3–4
The road makes a sharp bend to the left. Continue uphill past the trout farm – its fish is a Zaros speciality. After 15 minutes you reach small **Limni Votomos,** formed by the Zaros springs, with a good taverna on the south side.

4–5
Both the right- and left-hand paths lead round the shore of the lake and up stone steps. Go through the gate and proceed along the dirt path that ascends above the olive groves. As you round a bend you will see **Moni Agios Nikolaos** ahead on your left. Although the complex appears modern, the church has frescoes dating from the 14th century.

5–6
Opposite a little wooden bridge beside the monastery a set of rock steps on your right leads up to the tiny chapel of **Agios Efthimios,** filled with icons. Cross the bridge and follow the path as it turns sharply to the right and zigzags up and away from the monastery. Follow the yellow arrows and markings painted on the rocks to guide you through the boulders. You are now entering the **Faragi Rouvas (Rouvas Gorge),** which the locals also call Agios Nikolaos Gorge, after the monastery.

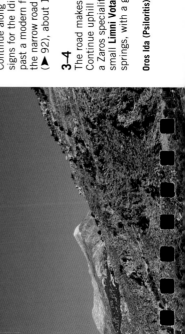

Oros Ida (Psiloritis) seen from Zaros

The church at Agios Nikolaos

6–7

After a short, steep climb you come to a fence. Go right, following the arrow as the path curves around the next hill. Take the stone steps up and through a gate. The 1.6km (1 mile) path through the gorge alternates easy stretches along the herb-covered hillsides with steeper climbs up stone steps. The route is well marked with yellow arrows.

7–8

The path follows the steep side of the gorge, then drops down through the ravine and doubles back on the far side. Here it becomes a wide track leading uphill to a signpost. To extend the walk to a full day, follow the trail up through the peaks for 2.7km (1.5 miles) to the mountain **church of Agios Ioannis**.

8–9

To return, follow the sign for Votamos and Agios Nikolaos. This dirt track is narrow and steep at first, so go slow. There are beautiful views down the gorge to Zaros. After passing some beehives turn left on to a wide dirt

road that leads downhill to the monastery. Follow the sign for Votamos round behind it to the wooden bridge, and return to Zaros the way you came.

Taking a Break

Taverna Oasis, opposite the post office in Zaros, is a cheerful spot. The Idi Hotel's pretty courtyard bar, the **Votamos Taverna** (➤ 94), and the **taverna** at Limni Votamos are other options.

Agios Ioannis

Faragi Rouvas

P s i l o r i t i s

1417m Samari

Moni Agios Nikolaos

Agios Efthimios

Limni Votamos

Idi Hotel

ZAROS

Oros Ida

1 km
½ mile

8
7
9
6
5
4
3
2
1

2 ORCHARDS & OLIVE GROVES

Walk

You will often see windmills from a distance while driving through Crete, but this walk enables you to view them up close. Following tracks and quiet roads, it links three of eastern Crete's unspoilt villages while meandering through olive groves and orchards of lemon trees, apple trees and bright red pomegranates.

DISTANCE 5km (3 miles)
TIME 2 hours
START/END POINT Limnes ✠ 185 D4

1–2

Driving west to east on the old road between Neapoli and Agios Nikolaos, pass the first few buildings as you arrive in Limnes and park just after a bridge on the right of the road at a sharp bend. Cross the bridge and walk along the path between white stone walls, past windmills and vines. After 50m (54 yards) reach a large taverna, where you turn left and immediately right. Pomegranate trees line one side of the path, olives and figs the other. Further on are patches of sweetcorn and cabbages, and lime and lemon trees.

2–3

At the next junction, turn left and immediately right again. The path is flanked with olive groves and passes, on the right, a red-roofed church surrounded by flowers and shrubs. The path goes slightly uphill as it brings you into Houmeriakos village, where you turn right, passing a shrine and a memorial on your right. In the village square there are a few cafés and shops. Take the road that goes uphill on the left side of the square, passing the church and an old fountain in a wall on your left.

3–4

Turn right at the first T-junction you reach, then follow the path as it swings left and climbs uphill. Pause on the corner for a view back to Limnes to the right, with the rest of the village of Houmeriakos to the left. From here carry on uphill, ignoring the track to the right. The main track then swings right and

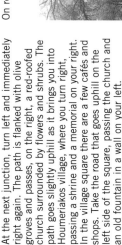

A grove of olive trees

carries on uphill, leaving the village behind. On reaching a tarmac road, turn right.

the village of Nikithianos, and to the right of that is Limnes, where the walk started. Up the hill to the immediate left is Vrises, your destination.

5–6

Continue on this quiet road until you reach a rough T-junction. The left fork leads up the long way round to the main Lasithiou–Neapoli road, and you can turn right into upper Vrises. If you turn right, however, it is an easy walk into lower Vrises, with its narrow streets and whitewashed houses with vine-covered terraces. To find a café or a shop you will need to pick your way up one of the sets of steps that leads up to the main part of the village. Afterwards, simply retrace your steps to Limnes where there are several tavernas.

TAKING A BREAK

There are simple tavernas and cafés in **Limnes, Houmeriakos** and **Vrises.**

4–5

The road swings right past more olive trees and heads towards a white chapel on a small hill. The chapel is locked but climb up to it for lovely views of the land around. Far to the left is Neapoli, to the right in the distance

3 OROPEDIO LASITHIOU

Drive

The Lasithiou Plateau stands 850m (2,790 feet) high in the Dikti Mountains, and is one of the most picturesque areas of the island. Orchards and olive groves cover the floors and slopes of the plateau.

DISTANCE 80km (50 miles) **TIME** 2–3 hours
START POINT Neapoli ⊞ 185 D4
END POINT Malia Archaeological Site ⊞ 184 C4

1–2
From the main square in Neapoli, follow the signs to the south for the "Plateau of Lasithiou" (sometimes spelt "Lassithi").
The route is well signed almost all the way.

The good tarmac road quickly winds up through olive groves and the upper part of the village of Vrises. After turning right, again signed, you'll see lovely views of the Selena Mountains ahead.

2–3
The road descends to irrigated olive groves then climbs up the other side of the little valley into a stark and rocky landscape. About 12km (7.5 miles) from Neapoli pass through the hamlet of Kato Amygdali, and soon

afterwards its big brother, Ano Amygdali.

After Ano Amygdali you reach the delightful village of Zenia, a cluster of vine-covered houses. At the far end of the village look for the spoon carver sitting outside his little house on the left.

3–4
The road winds higher now. Soon, on your right as you round a bend, you will see your first stone-based windmill. Next follows a series of small villages with women in traditional dress, donkeys with pack saddles, and villagers by the side of the road keen to sell you their honey, apples and *raki*.

4–5
The road gets increasingly steep as it crosses over the mountains, and in winter when it snows, this stretch may be closed. Beyond is

Poppies on the plateau

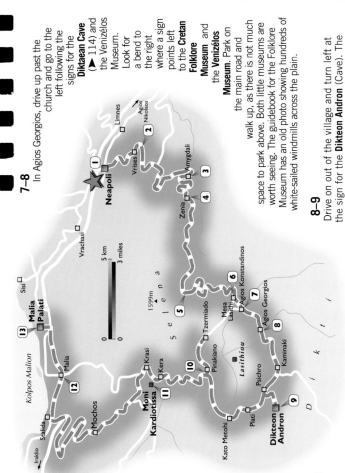

7–8

In Agios Georgios, drive up past the church and go to the left following the signs for the **Diktaean Cave** (▶ 114) and the Venizélos Museum. Look for a bend to the right where a sign points left to the **Cretan Folklore Museum** and the **Venizélos Museum**. Park on the main road and walk up above. Both little museums are worth seeing. The guidebook for the Folklore Museum has an old photo showing hundreds of white-sailed windmills across the plain.

8–9

Drive on out of the village and turn left at the sign for the **Dikteon Andron** (Cave). The

Looking for Zeus in the Dikteon Cave

the Lasithiou Plateau itself. As you descend there is a good view of the plots and fields on the flat central plain, and more villages to pass through where you'll find tavernas, shops and petrol stations.

6–7

After passing through Mesa Lasithi you reach a T-junction. Turn left towards Agios Georgios. The first village after the T-junction is Agios Konstandinos, where several shops sell weaving and textiles. From here, windmills start to appear in the fields.

The way of life is slow to change in Lasithiou

again, a pretty and majestic drive through a dry rocky landscape.

12–13
This road brings you into Malia a back way. Turn right at the stop sign towards Agios Nikolaos to reach the entrance to **Malia Palati** (▶ 102–103), a lovely place to end an impressive drive.

Metohi, the road splits. Ignore the left turn to Iraklio for the moment but carry straight on to Tzermiado, the largest town in the region. It's a pleasant old provincial town with handicrafts for sale and several restaurants. After a break you should return the way you came in, this time taking the road towards Iraklio.

10–11
Next follows one of the best parts of the drive, through the Perasma Seli Abelou (pass). Windmills can be seen along the ridge, to which you can walk if you want close-up views. As you descend from the pass, watch for the convent of **Moni Kardiotissa** (Our Lady of the Heart), on the outskirts of Kera on your left. The little stone church contains lovely 14th-century frescoes.

11–12
The road curves down the mountain – an exhilarating drive, but watch for the sharp right turn to Krasi. Look for the enormous gnarled old plane tree in the village, and the nearby spring where locals fill their water bottles. Carry on through the village and rejoin the main road, simply following signs now for Malia. The road curves back up over rocky hills, then switchbacks steeply back down

Taking a Break
Almost all the villages you pass through have tavernas and cafés. In Tzermiado, the **Restaurant Kri-Kri** (tel: 28440-22170) has good local food, and the **Kali Mera** (tel: 28440-31913), just west of Psichro, has simple food and great views. The **Platanos taverna**, beneath the plane tree at Krasi, is an atmospheric spot.

narrow road passes through more villages so take care when driving. Numerous tour buses use this route and the drivers are notoriously aggressive. Just beyond the town of Psychro, a sign points left up the hill 2km (1 mile) to the Dikteon Cave. There are more good views of the Lasithiou Plateau from the official car park.

9–10
Drive back down to Psychro and turn left, continuing the drive around the plateau. Orchards and farms are still plentiful, with olive groves and cows grazing on the plain. A few kilometres beyond the village of Kato

4 THE AMARI VALLEY

Drive

The Amari Valley is one of the most beautiful and fertile regions of Crete. Here you will enjoy breathtaking views, orchards, vineyards and olive groves, and experience genuine Cretan hospitality in the lovely villages encountered en route. You can start from Rethymno and join the route at Agia Fotini (31km/19 miles from Rethymno), thus missing the winding roads with spectacular views out of Agia Galini.

DISTANCE 100km (62 miles)
TIME 4–5 hours
START/END POINT Agia Galini ✚ 182 C2

1–2
Take the main road out of Agia Galini. Ignore the first two roads going off to the left. After 5km (3 miles) take the left turn for Amari and Rethymno. As you now head north you see the southern slopes of the Psiloritis range ahead of you to the right. After 2km (1 mile) a sign in Greek indicates the left turn to **Agia Paraskevi**, which you take. The road is asphalt but watch

Looking out over Amari town from the church tower

out for the pot-holes. Olive groves lie on either side, and high in the hills to your left is the mountain village of **Melampes.**

2–3
In Agia Paraskevi Ekklisia tis Panagias has fine 16th-century frescoes. You will have to park and ask for directions as it is hidden

away, off the main road. This road winds up through Agia Paraskevi and becomes more gravelly with sharp uphill bends. The high peak on the left on the far side of the valley is **Kedros** (1,776m/5,827 feet).

3–4
At the next junction take the left fork towards Rethymno. This is a wonderful road that snakes down into the valley and up the other side, with many a sharp bend. Look out for eagles and vultures circling overhead. Some 9km (5 miles) after the junction you reach an unmarked junction. Turn right and in 2km (1 mile) is the sleepy hamlet of Hordaki, and a few kilometres beyond that the hill town of **Ano Meros,** where white houses cover the hillside and there are a few cafés and shops.

4–5
About 4km (2.5 miles) beyond Ano Meros is **Vrises,** with more shops and cafés and, on the right of the main road, a large white war

memorial. These Amari Valley villages may look peaceful now, but after the kidnapping of the German General Kreipe during World War II (▶ 24), German troops destroyed them by way of reprisal, slaughtering the men, looting and burning the houses, and dynamiting schools and cemeteries. The villages were rebuilt after the war, although a few old churches survived.

The glorious Amari Valley spreads out below

5–6

About 5km (3 miles) after Vrises is **Gerakari,** the centre of the cherry-growing area. Stop at the Taverna Yerakari on the right of the main street to try cherry brandy or preserve. Other fruit and vegetables are preserved too. Food is served at meal times.

6–7

Continue through Gerakari, ignoring the left turn to Spili and various minor turns and staying on the main road towards **Meronas.** In Meronas look for the old church on the right. Park around the next bend where a monument commemorates the villagers who died in various wars from 1717 to 1949.

Walk back to look at the beautiful 14th-century Byzantine Ekklisia tis Panagias with its fresco-covered walls and ceilings.

7–8

A few kilometres beyond Meronas is a picnic stop on the right, with fabulous views of the valley. Soon after this is the village of Agia Fotini, where you meet a main road: turn right, signposted for the Asomati School. After 1km (0.5 miles) turn left for **Thronos.**

8–9

In Thronos is the wonderful 11th-century Ekklisia tis Panagias, on the right. Though it is usually locked, part of a lovely mosaic can be seen

11–12

At **Apodoulou**, if time allows, park in the village and look for the signs to the Minoan site, which is still being excavated, and to the 14th-century Church of Agios Georgios.

12–13

Beyond Apodoulou, ignore the left fork marked Platanos and keep on the main road to the right (not signed). Rejoin the main road and turn left towards Timpaki, then at the next junction turn right back to Agia Galini.

TAKING A BREAK

There are numerous options, the best for a meal being the **Taverna Yerakari** and the **Noukakis** in Amari.

Byzantine church in the valley

on the floor outside the church, and beyond it good views of the valley.

9–10

Beyond Thronos the road forks. Turn right to loop back down and meet the main road again, where you turn left. When you reach the next few houses take the sharp right turn to the village of **Amari** itself. In Amari, park in the small square outside the taverna and walk up the nearby narrow street that heads

up towards the Venetian bell tower. You can climb the tower to enjoy the views but there is no guardrail, so take care. Drive out of the village square the way you came in, keeping straight on past the police station and on through Monastiraki to rejoin the main road.

10–11

At the main road turn right, signposted Vizari. Drive on through Vizari to Fourfouras. Continue through Fourfouras and Kouroutes and, as you leave the next village, Nithavris, take the road to Timpaki, ignoring the right turn to Agios Ioannis.

War memorials stand in every village

5 WEST COAST OF CRETE

Drive

Some of Crete's best sandy beaches lie on the island's far western coast, and their remote location has so far brought only minimal development, leaving them largely unspoiled. The dramatic mountain and coastal scenery is well worth the long day's drive. Drive with care on the narrow mountain roads.

DISTANCE 110km (68 miles)
TIME 3 hours driving, 5 hours with stops
START/END POINT Kastelli Kissamos (43km/27 miles west of Chania) ⊞ 180 B4

1–2

From Kastelli Kissamos on the north coast, take the Old Road east towards Chania for about 2km (1.2 miles) to Kaloudiana. Turn south to **Topolia**, a pretty whitewashed village clinging to steep slopes. The church of Agia Paraskevi, with its striking Italianate bell tower, has late Byzantine frescoes.

Top right: In the Agia Sofia cave

2–3

Just beyond town a single-lane tunnel marks the start of the **Koutsomatados ravine**. Only 1.5km (1 mile) long, it is highly dramatic, the narrow road clinging to the western slope with sheer cliffs rising 300m (984ft) above a river bed. Near the end of the gorge, steep steps on the right lead up to **Agia Sofia** cave, one of the biggest on Crete. The huge cavern is filled with stalagmites and stalactites, and there is

a small chapel. It was occupied in neolithic times. Just beyond is **Koutsomatados** village with a couple of tavernas.

3–4

Continue straight ahead on the main road through the Tiflos Valley, lush with olive groves and tall plane and chestnut trees.

4–5

At **Elos**, the road winds up the hillside to the centre of this pretty village, the

largest of the nine *kastanochoria*, or chestnut villages, which export the crop A chestnut festival is held here in late October.

5–6

As you climb higher out of Elos, look back at the spectacular views over the valley and its terraced hillsides. Pass Perivolia, and at the T-junction turn left for Elafonisi. The road curves down a pretty, peaceful valley, passing through **Vathi**, another chestnut village, and **Plokamiana.**

6–7

A good asphalt road enables a fast descent to the sea, 10km (6 miles) away with a scenic rocky shoreline. Perched on a rock bluff above the barren landscape is **Moni Chrysoskalitisas.** The convent's name

means "Virgin of the Golden Step", as one of the 90 steps up to it is said to be made of gold (visible only to those who are without sin). The original church was built in a cave in the 13th century. This one dates from the 19th century and contains an ancient icon of the Virgin.

7–8

It's a further 6km (4 miles) to the silver-grey sands of **Elafonisi**, at the southwestern

tip of the island. The paved road ends after 4km (2.5 miles), and a rough gravel track leads down to the beach. The turquoise waters are warm and shallow, seldom reaching above waist height, and you can wade across the sandbar to **Elafonisi Island.** Despite its remoteness, this idyllic spot is always busy in high season; there are a few snack bars and plenty of sunbeds for hire.

8–9

Return on the same road, and after Vathi take the left fork through **Kefali.** Its 14th-century church, Metamorphosis tou Sotirou (Transfiguration of the Saviour), contains fine Byzantine frescoes as well as graffiti from early travellers. A path beside the *kafeníon* leads to the church.

9–10

Beyond the next village, tiny Papadiana, the road becomes a series of tight, narrow switchbacks climbing up the mountainside. It's very windy here so take care. Look back across the valley for stunning views of the glistening sea. After Amygdalokefali, wide vistas of the western coast open out as the long, slow descent begins through old

Topola ②
Kalathenes
Agia Sofia ③
Koutsomatados ④
Tiflos
Rogdia
Melissia
890m
Manna
Sfinari
O Sfinari
Afrotolaki
Kampos
Keramoti ⑩
Papadiana
Amygdalokefali
Kefali ⑨
Vathi
Perivolia
Elos ⑤
Tzitzifia
Plokamiana
⑥
O Stomiou
⑦
Moni Chrysoskalitisas
⑧
Elafonisi
⑪

0 5 km
0 3 miles

mountain villages such as Keramoti. You only realise how high you are when you glimpse the sea and the coastal fields far below.

10–11

Kampos, 14km (9 miles) from Kefali, is a pleasant village with ruined stone houses clinging to the slopes around a ravine. After winding through it you make a magnificent descent into the canyon lined with rock walls of red and gold covered in greenery, and on to **Sfinari**, known for its thyme honey.

11–12

The road climbs again, affording a stupendous view over the bay and beach below. The big peak of Mount Manna looms ahead. After 9km (6 miles) turn left for **Platanos**, a large town of sandstone houses perched on a high plateau. Drive through town. Most signs are in Greek only, making the ill-marked turn for Falassarna more difficult to see (it's better signposted from the other direction). As you leave town look for a blue BANK sign. Turn left on to the small road here. Shortly after the turn follow the brown and yellow sign for Ancient

Sand and dunes at Falassarna

Falassarna. As you descend to the coastal plain, turn right at the signposted junction for Falassarna.

12–13

Falassarna has lovely stretches of golden sand set between rocky inlets that are great for beachcombing. Facilities are basic, with a handful of small hotels and tavernas scattered along the road. North of the beach a rough, rocky track leads to the ruins of ancient Falassarna, a port city dating back to the 6th century. Return to Platanos and continue north to Kastelli, 11km (7 miles) away.

TAKING A BREAK

The **Kastanofolia taverna** in Elos serves good food. There are snack bars with drinks and sandwiches at Elafonisi. On the coast road the larger villages of Kampos and Sfinari have tavernas. The **Sun Set taverna** at Falassarna is a simple but pleasant spot. Most are closed out of season, so take a picnic lunch.

ΟΔΟΣ
25 ΗΣ ΑΥΓΟΥΣΤΟΥ

IONIAN
BANK

Practicalities

BEFORE YOU GO

WHAT YOU NEED

	Some countries require a passport to remain valid for a minimum period (usually at least six months) beyond the date of entry – check before booking	UK	Germany	USA	Canada	Australia	Ireland	Netherlands	Spain
● Required ○ Suggested ▲ Not required									
Passport/National Identity Card		●	●	●	●	●	●	●	●
Visa (regulations can change – check before booking)		▲	▲	▲	▲	▲	▲	▲	▲
Onward or Round-Trip Ticket		▲	▲	▲	▲	▲	▲	▲	▲
Health Inoculations (tetanus and polio)		▲	▲	▲	▲	▲	▲	▲	▲
Health Documentation (▶ 190, Health)		▲	▲	▲	▲	▲	▲	▲	▲
Travel Insurance		○	○	○	○	○	○	○	○
Driver's License (national)		●	●	●	●	●	●	●	●
Car Insurance Certificate		●	●	●	●	●	●	●	●
Car Registration Document		●	●	●	●	●	●	●	●

WHEN TO GO

Peak season   Off-season

JAN	FEB	MAR	APR	MAY	JUN	JUL	AUG	SEP	OCT	NOV	DEC
12°C	12°C	14°C	17°C	21°C	23°C	25°C	26°C	25°C	21°C	17°C	14°C
54°F	54°F	57°F	63°F	70°F	73°F	77°F	79°F	77°F	70°F	63°F	57°F

Very wet   Wet   Cloud   Sun   Sun/Showers

April and May are probably the best two months to visit, when temperatures are pleasant without being too hot, there is very little rain, the island is not yet too busy and there is a profusion of wild flowers to see. **September and October** can also be pleasant, but more suited to swimmers than botanists. The landscape will be looking burnt out, but the sea temperatures will still be in the low 20s(°C)/mid-70s(°F). In **July and August** there is no rain at all. Temperatures remain mild all through the year, but in winter it does get wet, it can drop down to freezing in the mountains at night, and it can snow, even by the sea. The holiday season usually runs from **April to October**. Outside this period many hotels and restaurants close. Some open all year round, but your choice is limited.

GETTING ADVANCE INFORMATION

Websites
● www.explorecrete.com
● www.infocrete.com
● www.interkriti.org
● www.cretetravel.com
● www.gnto.gr

In the UK
Greek National Tourism
Organisation (GNTO)
4 Conduit Street
London W15 2DJ
☎ 020 7495 9300

In the USA
Greek National Tourism
Organisation (GNTO)
645 Fifth Avenue
New York, NY 10022
☎ (212) 421-5777

GETTING THERE

By Air Crete has two international airports, at **Iraklio** and **Chania**, although the one at Iraklio is the major airport and much more frequently used. They are about two hours apart by road, with Iraklio best for eastern Crete and Chania for western Crete, There is also an airport at **Sitia** (▶ 36) in eastern Crete, which handles domestic flights and a handful of international flights (largely charters).

There are **numerous charter flights** from various European airports from April to October and outside these times there are fights to Larnaca and Rome with Aegean. Most scheduled flights involve flying to Athens and changing there to another flight. There are 20 to 30 flights a day from Athens to Crete in season, with the national carrier Olympic Airways and Aegean Airlines. There are also air links with Rhodes and Thessaloniki.

By Sea From **Piraeus** in Athens there are daily ferry services in summer to **Iraklio**, **Chania** and **Rethymno**, and several a week to **Agios Nikolaos** and Sitia. Journey time is about 12 hours, or less in good weather. There is also a fast ferry with Minoan Lines, which cuts the journey time to between 6 and 7 hours. There are also numerous other connections to Crete: from Githio on the Peloponnese, from Thira (Santorini) and other Cycladic islands, from Rhodes, Karpathos and other Dodecanesian islands, and from Israel, Cyprus and Egypt.

Bear in mind that ferry schedules can often be affected by stormy or windy weather, not only off the coast of Crete itself but throughout the Aegean. This applies as much in high summer, when winds can be strong, as at any other time of year. Always leave at least a day's grace if you need to connect to onward flights or ferries.

TIME

Like the rest of Greece, Crete is two hours ahead of Greenwich Mean Time (GMT+2), and adjusts to summer time at 4am on the last Sunday in March until 4am on the last Sunday in October.

CURRENCY AND FOREIGN EXCHANGE

Currency The monetary unit of Crete is the Euro (€). Euro notes are in denominations of €5, €10, €20, €50, €100, €200 and €500, and coins in denominations of €1 and €2, and 1, 2, 5, 10, 20 and 50 cents. Other currencies such as the US dollar and the pound sterling can still be widely exchanged.

Credit and debit cards Credit and debit cards are widely accepted in the resorts and ATMs are common in large towns and cities.

Exchange Cash and travellers' cheques can be exchanged in banks and at exchange bureaux. Post offices in Greece no longer offer currency exchange facilities. Banks generally give the best exchange rates, although commission charges can vary quite a bit from bank to bank, so shop around.New York. If your bank is not US-based, check before you travel to make sure your PIN number will work in New York.

In Greece	**In Canada**	**In Australia**
Greek National Tourism Organisation (GNTO) Tsoha 7, Athens 11521 ☎ (210) 870 7000	Hellenic Tourism, 1500 Don Mills Road, Suite 102, Toronto, ON M3B 3K4 ☎ (416) 968-2220	GNTO 37–49 Pitt Street, Sydney, NSW 2000 ☎ 02 9241 1663

WHEN YOU ARE THERE

CLOTHING SIZES

U.K.	Greece	U.S.A.		
36	46	36		
38	48	38		
40	50	40		
42	52	42		Suits
44	54	44		
46	56	46		
7	41	8		
7.5	42	8.5		
8.5	43	9.5		
9.5	44	10.5		Shoes
10.5	45	11.5		
11	46	12		
14.5	37	14.5		
15	38	15		
15.5	39/40	15.5		
16	41	16		Shirts
16.5	42	16.5		
17	43	17		
8	34	6		
10	36	8		
12	38	10		
14	40	12		Dresses
16	42	14		
18	44	16		
4.5	38	6		
5	38	6.5		
5.5	39	7		
6	39	7.5		Shoes
6.5	40	8		
7	41	8.5		

NATIONAL HOLIDAYS

1 Jan	New Year's Day
6 Jan	Epiphany
Feb/Mar	Shrove Monday (41 days pre-Easter)
25 Mar	Independence Day
Mar/Apr	Good Friday, Easter Monday
May/Jun	Whit Monday (50 days after Easter)
1 May	Labour Day
15 Aug	Feast of the Assumption
28 Oct	Ochi Day
25/26 Dec	Christmas

Restaurants and tourist shops may well stay open on these days, but museums will be closed.

OPENING HOURS

○ Stores   ● Post Offices
● Offices   ● Museums/Monuments
● Banks   ● Pharmacies

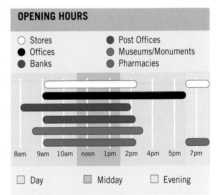

8am 9am 10am noon 1pm 2pm 4pm 5pm 7pm

☐ Day   ▨ Midday   ☐ Evening

Many shops in tourist areas stay open late. In larger towns, some banks and post offices may open on Saturday mornings.

Pharmacies These are normally open weekdays only, but some open on Saturdays and each one displays details of the nearest 24-hour pharmacy.

Churches Churches are often open all day, though some may open early morning and evenings only.

Museums Museum hours vary from place to place. It is advisable to check, especially if travelling out of season or making a special journey.

TIME DIFFERENCES

GMT	Crete	New York	Germany	Spain	Australia
12 noon	→ 2pm	← 7am	→ 1pm	→ 1pm	→ 10pm

PERSONAL SAFETY

Crete is one of the safest places in Europe. Crime is rare, although petty theft can occur so don't be too careless with your valuables. Report any crime to the police immediately.

- Leave valuables in your hotel or apartment safe, never on the beach or visible in a car.

- Women may be pestered by local lotharios, but these are usually a nuisance rather than a serious threat. Persistent refusal usually works.

Police assistance:
☎ **100** from any phone

TELEPHONES

calling. You will use the street kiosks. Simply dial and pay the attendant at the end according to the meter.

For the domestic operator dial 151. For the international operator dial 161, or 162 from Athens. The cheapest way to call internationally is at one of the OTE offices.

To make a call from a street phone you must have a phone card, available at numeous outlets. Otherwise and number you are

International Dialling Codes
Dial 00 followed by

UK:	44
USA/Canada:	1
Ireland:	353
Australia:	61
Germany:	49

POST OFFICES

Towns and many large villages have a post office, either in a large yellow caravan or a building on the main square or street. Normal hours are Mon–Fri 7:30–2:30, but in main towns and busy tourist resorts they may stay open until 8pm, and also open Saturday mornings.

ELECTRICITY

The power supply in Greece is 220. Sockets take two-round-pin plugs. Visitors from continental Europe should bring an adaptor. Visitors from the US will require a voltage transformer. Power cuts happen from time to time.

TIPS/GRATUITIES

Tipping is expected for all services. As a general guide:

Restaurant waiters (service not included)	leave change
Cafés/bars	leave change
Taxis	change from bill
Porters	€1– €3 per bag
Chambermaids	€2 per day (optional)
Hairdressers	change from bill
Tour guides	€3

POLICE 100	
FIRE 199	
AMBULANCE 166	
ELPA (CAR BREAKDOWN) 104	

HEALTH

 Insurance Citizens of EU countries receive free or reduced-cost emergency medical treatment with relevant documentation (European Helath Insurance Card), but private medical insurance is still advised and essential for all other visitors.

 Dental Services There are many good dentists in Crete, mostly in the major towns of Iraklio, Chania and Rethymno. Services are much cheaper than elsewhere in Europe.

 Weather The summer sun can be fierce, and even in spring and autumn you must take precautions against sunburn. Even if there is some cloud cover, still use protection as the rays and reflections will burn.

 Drugs Prescription and non-prescription drugs are widely available at pharmacies. Look for the Green Cross. Pharmacies work a rota system out of hours and will have a notice indicating the nearest open one. Bring sufficient supplies of any medication with you, plus a prescription indicating generic and not brand names in case you need more. Be aware that codeine is banned in Greece, so check the contents of any medical supplies in case you fall foul of the law.

Safe Water Tap water is safe to drink throughout Crete. Bottled water is available everywhere. Drink plenty to avoid dehydration in the hot summer months.

CONCESSIONS

Students/Youths Students Holders of an International Student Identity Card (ISIC) are entitled to reduced-price admission at most public museums and monuments. Privately run museums may not give a concession. No travel concessions available.

Senior Citizens Senior citizens receive few if any concessions. Some sites and museums will offer reduced admission if you can prove you are over 60. Sometimes this is limited to EU citizens. No travel concessions are available.

TRAVELING WITH A DISABILITY

Crete is not ideal, so check first if your accommodation is going to be suitable. Few special facilities exist, and archaeological sites are difficult to get around. That said, Cretans are always willing to help anyone in need so the personal touch may see you through.

CHILDREN

Cretans love children and they are welcome everywhere. You will often see a group of Greek children eating at one table while the adults dine together at another. Children under 8 travel free on buses, but over-8s pay full fare.

RESTROOMS

Standards vary. Most people prefer to use a bar or café toilet, and proprietors don't usually mind. Remember not to put the paper into the toilet, but into the basket provided. stores.

WILDLIFE SOUVENIRS

The import of wildlife souvenirs sourced from rare or endangered species may be illegal or require a special permit. Before buying, check your home country's customs regulations.

CONSULATES

UK	Ireland	Germany	Australia	Netherlands
2810-224012	(010)721 2951	28210-68876	(210) 8704000	2810-343299
	(Athens)	(Chania)	(Athens)	

THE GREEK ALPHABET

Alpha A α
Vita B β
Gamma Γ γ
Delta Δ δ
Epsilon Ε ε
Zita Ζ ζ
Eta Η η
Thita Θ θ
Iota Ι ι
Kappa Κ κ
Lambda Λ λ
Mi Μ μ
Ni Ν ν
Xi Ξ ξ
Omicron O o
Pi Π π
Rho Ρ ρ
Sigma Σ σ
Taf Τ τ
Upsilon Υ υ
Phi Φ φ
Chi Χ χ
Psi Ψ ψ
Omega Ω ω

TRAVEL

Airport **Aerodhrómio**
Harbour **Limáni**
Bus station **Stathmós leoforión**
Bus stop **Stási**
Bus **Leoforío**
Car **Aftokínito**
Taxi **Taxí**

DAYS OF THE WEEK

Monday **Deftéra**
Tuesday **Trití**
Wednesday **Tetárti**
Thursday **Pémpti**
Friday **Paraskeví**
Saturday **Sávato**
Sunday **Kyriakí**

OTHER USEFUL WORDS & PHRASES

Good morning **Kaliméra**
Good afternoon/evening **Kalispéra**
Good night **Kaliníkhta**
Okay, all right **Endáksi**
Very well **Polí kalá**
I'm fine **Kalá iméh**
I think so **Nomízo**
I'm not too bad **Étsi kyétsi**
Enjoy your meal **Kalí órexi**
Cheers! **(Stín) yía más**
What can I do for you? **Oríste?**
What's your name? **Pos sas léne**
Be careful **Prosexteh**
Take your time **Sigá sigá**
Who **Pyós**
What **Ti**
When **Póte**
Why **Yiatí**
How **Pos**
How much? **Póses/Pósi/Pósa**
How many? **Póses?**
A little **Lígho**
Open **Aníkhto**
Closed **Klistó**

SURVIVAL PHRASES

Yes (formal) **Ne (málista)**
No **Óchi**
Hello (formal) **Yiásas (hérete)**
Goodbye (formal) **Yiásas (adío)**
How are you? **Ti kanís (tí káneteh)?**
Please **Parakaló**
Thank you (very much) **Efharistó (párapolí)**
Excuse me **Signómi**
I'm sorry **Signómi**
You're welcome **Parakaló**
Do you have...? **Boríte na moú dósete...?**
How much? **Póso íneh?**

DIRECTIONS

Where is...? **Poú íne...?**
    - the beach **i paralía**
    - the bank **i trápeza**
    - the bus stop **io stási**
    - the church **i eklissía**
    - the post office **to tachidrómio**
    - the hospital **to nosokomío**
    - the hotel **to xenodohío**
    - the sea **i thálassa**
    - the telephone **to tiléfono**
    - the toilet **i toualéta**

Left **Aristerá**   Right **Deksiá**
Straight on **Ísia**
How far is it? **Póso makriá íneh?**
Near **Kondá**   Far **Makriá**

NUMBERS

0 midhén	14 dhekatéssera	40 saránda	600 exakósia
1 éna	15 dhekapénde	50 penínda	700 eftakósia
2 dhío	16 dhekaéxi	60 exínda	800 ochtakósia
3 tría	17 dhekaeftá	70 evdhomínda	900 enyakósia
4 téssera	18 dhekaochtó	80 oghdhónda	
5 pénde	19 dhekaenyá	90 enenínda	1,000 hílya
6 éxi	20 íkosi	100 ekató	
7 eftá		110 ekató dhéka	
8 ochtó	21 íkosi éna	120 ekatón íkosi	
9 enyá	22 íkosi dhío		
10 dhéka	30 tr`ianda	200 dhiakósia	
11 éndheka	31 tríanda éna	300 triakósia	
12 dhódheka	32 tríanda dhío	400 tetrakósia	
13 dhekatría		500 pendakósia	

IF YOU NEED HELP

Help! **Voíthya!**
Could you help me, please? **Boríte na me voithísete, parakaló?**
Do you speak English? **Miláte angliká?**
I don't understand **Dhen katalavéno**
Could you call/fetch a doctor quickly, please? **Parakaló, kaléste/idhopíste ghríghora éna yatró?**
Could I use your telephone? **Boró na chrisimopiíso to tiléfono sas?**
Police **Astinomía**
Ambulance **Asthenofóro**

TIME

What time is it?
Ti óra íne?
Today **Símera**
Tomorrow **Ávrio**
Yesterday **Kthés**
In the morning
To proí
In the afternoon
To mesiméri
In the evening
To vrádhi
At night **io níchta**

DRIVING

Petrol **Venzíni**
– unleaded
amólivdhi
Fill **yemízo**
Petrol station
Venzinádhiko
Diesel **Dízel**
Oil **Ládhi**
Tyre **Lásticho**
Garage **Garáz**

RESTAURANT (ESTIATÓRIO)

Can I book a table **Boró na klíso éna trapézi**
A table for two **Éna trapézi yía dhío átoma**
Can we eat outside? **Boróome na fáme kyéxo?**
Could we see the menu/wine list?
Boróome na dhóome ton gatálogho/ton gatálogho krasyón?
Could I have the bill please?
To loghariazmó, parakaló?

MENU READER

bíra beer
chortofághos vegetarian
vradhinó dinner
gála milk
hórta wild greens
kafés coffee
– **nescafé** instant
karáfa carafe
krasí wine
– **áspro** white
– **kókkino** red
– **kokkinélli** rosé
kréas meat
khimós fruit juice
neró water

orektikó hors d'oeuvre
proinó breakfast
psitó grilled
tighanitó fried
tsai tea
voútiro butter
vrazméno boiled

MENU A–Z

afélia pork cubes cooked in a red wine and coriander sauce
aláti salt
anginári artichoke
angoúri cucumber
antsóoya anchovy
avgó egg
avgolémono egg and lemon soup
baklává pastry filled with nuts and honey
banána banana
dolmádes minced meat and rice wrapped in vine leaves
domátes tomatoes
eliés olives
eleóladho olive oil
fakés lentils
fasólia beans
fétta goat's cheese
glyká fruit in sweet syrup
haloúmi ewe's cheese
hirómeri cured ham
húmmos chickpea dip
kalambhóki sweetcorn
karóto carrot
keftédhes meatballs
kerásya cherries
kétsap tomato sauce
kléftiko oven-baked lamb
kolokitháki courgette
koniák brandy
kounoupídhi cauliflower
kotópoulo chicken
kounélli rabbit
krém karamél crème caramel
kremídhi onion
láchano cabbage
ládhi salad oil
lemóni lemon
loukániko sausage
loúntza smoked pork loin
makaróhya spaghetti

mandaríni mandarin
manitária mushrooms
maroúli lettuce
melitzána aubergine
mídhya mussels
milópita apple pie
moussakás minced meat, aubergine, potatoes, etc, in a bechamel sauce
paidháki lamb chop
pagotó ice-cream
patátes potatoes
pepóni melon
pikándiko spicy
pipéri pepper
piperyá pepper (vegetable)
pítta flat bread
portokáli orange
pourgoúri cracked wheat
psári fish
psomí bread
saláta salad
sáltza sauce
sardhéles sardines
skórdho garlic
soujoúkos almonds in grape juice
soúpa soup
souvláki grilled meat on skewer
spanáki spinach
stafília grapes
stifádho beef stewed in onion and tomato sauce
seftaliá lamb sausage
tahini sesame seed dip
taramosalata fish-roe dip
vodhinó kréas beef
yaoúrti yoghurt
zambón ham

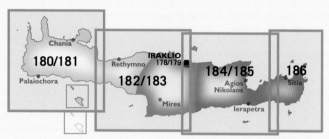

To identify the regions, see the
map on the inside of the front cover

Streetplan 178-179

Main road/minor road
Other road
City wall
Important building

Featured place of interest
Other place of interest
† Church
Park/garden

Regional Maps

Major route
Motorway
Main road
Secondary road
Minor road
National park

□ Town/village
✈ Airport
Featured place of interest
Other place of interest

```
180–186    0        10 km
           0     5 miles
```

Atlas

Iraklio/Heraklion

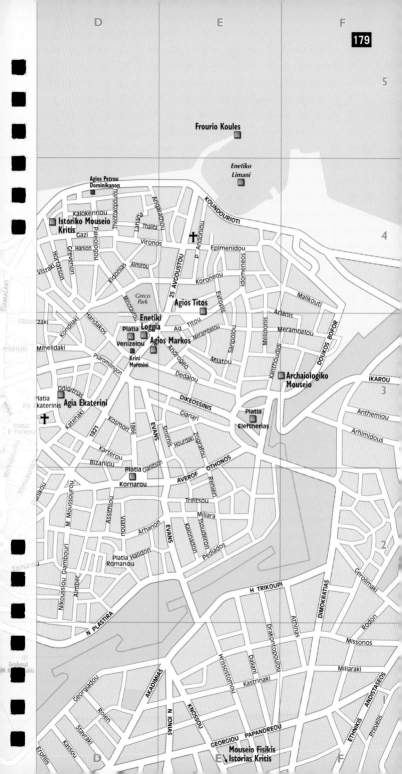

Frourio Koules

Enetiko Limani

Agios Petrou Dominikanon

Kalokerinou
Istoriko Mouseio Kritis
Gazi
Paleologou
Hanion

Theotokopoulou
Lahana
Thalita
Vironos
Anapnatnou
Andonifou

KOUNDOURIOTI

Epimenidou
Almirou
Kidonias
25 AVGOUSTOU
Koroneou

Greco Park

Vistaki
Hortatson
Hanion
Grevenon
Kondilaki
Handakos
Minoarou

Enetiki Loggia
Platia Venizelou
Agios Markos
Krini Morosini

Agios Titos
Ag. Titou
Merambelou
Androgeo
Dedalou
Milatou

Evropis
Idomeneos

Malikouti
Arianis
Merambelou
Sarpidou
Melidonis
Xanthoudidi

DOUKOS BOFOR

Archaiologiko Mouseio

IKAROU

Minelidaki
Psaromiligkon

Agia Ekaterini
Odiditrias
Platia Ag. Ekaterinis
Katehaki
1821
Kosmon
1866
Karterou
Bizaniou

DIKEOSSINIS
Gianari
Smirnis
Hourdaki
Zografou

Platia Eleftherias

Anthemiou
Arhimidous

Gialkou
Platia Kornarou
Gianitson
AVEROF
OTHONOS
Renieri
Trifitsou
Miliara
Tsouideron
Kalinhadon
Pediados

M. Moussson
Assithiou
Vianou
Arhanon
EVANS

Platia Halidon Romanou

Nikousjou Giambouri
Amber

H TRIKOUPI
Drakontopoulou
Athinas
DIMOKRATIAS
Gerolimaki
Rodon
Missonos
Miliaraki

N PLASTIRA

Georgiadou
Rojen
Stavraki
Kassou
Eroilis

AKADIMIAS
N IONIAS
KNOSSOU
GEORGIOU PAPANDREOU
Hrissostomou
Kastrinaki
Dailani

ETNIKIS ANDISTASEOS
Prevelis

Mouseio Fisikis Istorias Kritis

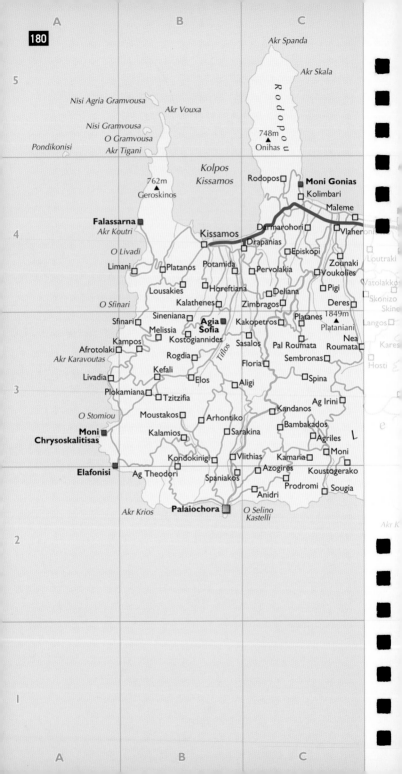

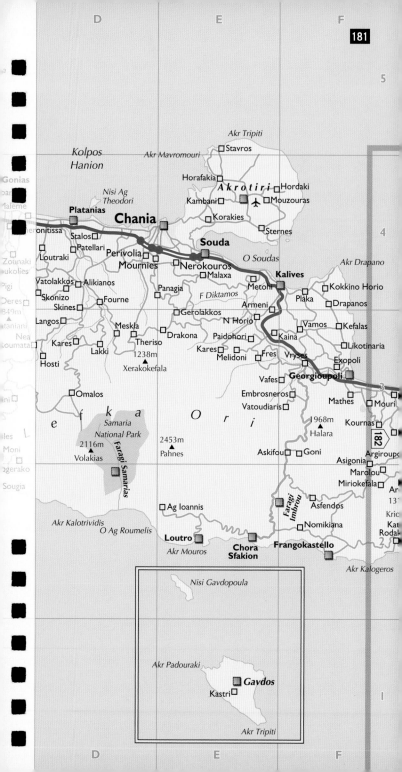

Kolpos
Hanion

Akr Mavromouri

Akr Tripiti

Stavros

Horafakia

A k r o t i r i   Hordaki

Kambani   Mouzouras

Nisi Ag Theodori

Platanias

Korakies

Chania   Sternes

eronitissa   Souda

Stalos   *O Soudas*

Loutraki   Patellari   Perivolia   Nerokouros   Kalives   *Akr Drapano*

Mournies   Malaxa   Metohi   Kokkino Horio

Vatolakkos   Alikianos   Panagia   Plaka   Drapanos

Skonizo   *F Diktamos*   Armeni

Deres   Fourne   Gerolakkos   N Horio   Vamos   Kefalas

Skines   Paidohori   Kaina   Likotinaria

Langos   Meskla   Kares   Fres   Exopoli

Nea   Drakona   Melidoni   Vryses

oumata   Kares   Theriso   Georgioupoli   Mouri

Lakki   1238m   Xerakokefala   Vafes

Hosti   Embrosneros   Mathes

Omalos   Vatoudiaris   Kournas

e   *f*   *k*   *a*   *O*   *r*   *i*   1968m   Halara

Samaria   National Park   2453m   Askifou   Goni   Asigonia

2116m   Pahnes   Marolou

Volakias   Miriokefala

Ag Ioannis   Asfendos

Akr Kalotrividis   Nomikiana

O Ag Roumelis   Loutro   Chora   Frangokastello

Akr Mouros   Sfakion   *Akr Kalogeros*

Faragi Samarias   *Faragi Imbrou*

Gonias   Maleme

Zounaki   oukolies

Pigi   atianiani

les   Moni   ogerako   Sougia

182   Argiroupc   13   Kric   Kat   Rodak   Ar

Nisi Gavdopoula

Akr Padouraki

Gavdos

Kastri

Akr Tripiti

5

A   B   C

Akr Drapano

ckino Horio

apanos

Kefalas

Ormos
Almirou

Likotinaria

kopoli

4   Gerani

Rethymno

Panormos

Skaleta

Ahlades

Angelliana

Prinos

Platanias

Pigi

Perama

Viranepiskopi

Kirianna

Margarites

Dramia   Prines

Kato
Valsamonero

Mili

Ag Triada

Roupes

Mouri

Eleftherna

ches

Episkopi

Somatas

Prasies

Kalandar

Kournas

Ag Andreas

Kinigiana

Ag

Patima

Armeni

Kavousi

Moni
Arkadiou

181

Selli

Argiroupoli   Roustika

Filakio

asigonia   Ano Malaki

Fotinos

d

15

Marolou

Velonado

Koumi

Geni

Thronos

Vistagi

Miriokefala

Arolithi

Alones

Karines

Agia Fotini

Or
Fourfour

1312m   Ag Ioannis

Amari

Krioneritis

Koxare

Monastiraki

Kato
Rodakino

Sellia

Atsipades

Spili

Gerakari

Vizari

3   Mariou   Mourne   e

Plakias   Frati   Kissos

Ano Meros   Ni
Ap

O Plakia   Drimiskos   Kendrohori

Akr Kalogeros   Akr Kakomouri   Damnoni   Giannou   Akoumia

Moni Preveli   Preveli   1136m   Orne   Platis

Siderotas

Melampes   Klim

Ag Pavlos   Agia Galini   Kokkinos
Pirgos

Akr Melissa

2   Ormos
Mesaras   Kalama

Nisi Paximadia   Akr
M

1

A   B   C

5

4

3

2

Akr Korakias

Akr Stavros

O Fodele

Akr Korakia

Kolpos
Irakliou

Akr Panagia

Bali

**Spilaio
Melidoniou**

Melidoni

Agia

Geropotamos

Ag Silas

Kalandare

Ag Mamas

Livadia

Zoniana

1575m
Sitaras

2456m

Oros Psiloritis

Fourfouras

**Ideon
Andron**

1920m
Alikadam

Nithavris

Apodoulou

Platanos

Kamares

Magarikari

Klima

Lagolio

Kissi

Timpaki

Vori

**Mouseio
Kritikis
Ethnologias**

Galia

**Agia
Triada**

Kamilari

Ag Ioannis

Kalamaki

Petrokefali

Pitsidia

Sivas

Pombia

Matala

Pigaidakia

Akr
Matala

Andiskari

Kali Limenes

Akr Lithino

Kokkinos
Pirgos

Phaistos

Mires

Alithini

Plora

Platanos

Geropotamos

Vasiliki

Koumasa

Krotos

Lendas

Gerokambos

Sises

Aloïdes

Doxarou

Garazo

Veni

Axos

Anogia

Honos

Aidonohori

Gonies

1199m
Voskero

Korfes

Krousonas

Kato Asites

Kerasia

Zaros

Moroni

Gergeri

Ano Moulia

Kato Moulia

Inia

Valis

Gortys

Agioi Deka

Vagionia

Loukia

Loures

Asimi

Kapetaniana

Akr Martelos

Ag Pelagia

Ahlada

Fodele

Rogdia

Marathos

Arolithos

Tilisos

Voutes

Stavrakia

Ag Mironas

Dafnes

Venerato

Afgeniki

Ag Thomas

Megali Vrisi

Larani

Ag Sillas

Iraklio

Gazi

**Mouseio Fysikis
Istorias Kritis**

Kavrohori

Kato Kalesa

Knossos

Silamo

Pano
Arhanes

Prof
Ilias

Kiparissos

Houdet

Karkadiotis

Genna

Metaxohori

Melidohori

Tefeli

Ligortino

Faragiana

Sternes

Harakas

Paranir

Platanias

Tris Ek

184

Pi

Kouloukonas

Psiloritis

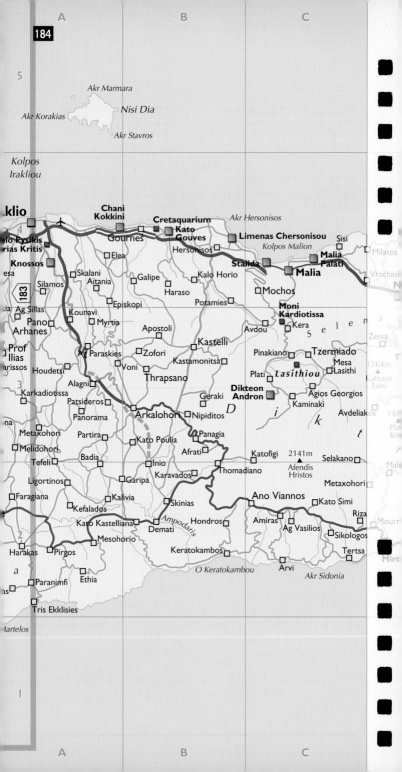

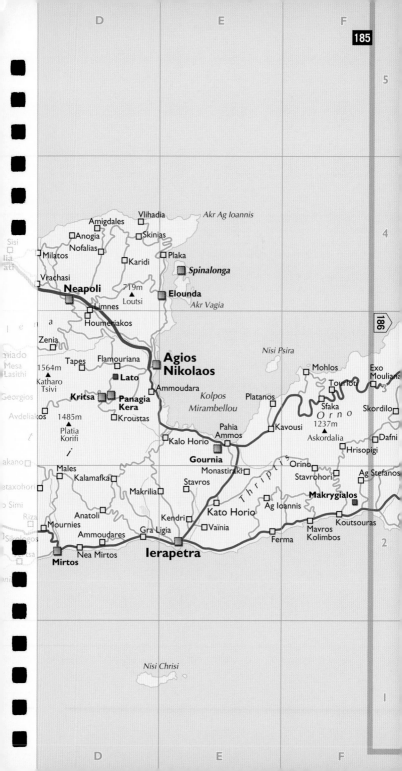

186

D

E

F

5

4

2

1

Sisi
lia
ati

Akr Ag Ioannis

Vlihadia

Amigdales

Anogia

Skinias

Nofalias

Milatos

Karidi

Plaka

Spinalonga

Vrachasi

Neapoli

Elounda

719m
Loutsi

Akr Vagia

Limnes

Houmeriakos

a

Zenia

n a

Nisi Psira

niado
Mesa
Lasithi

Tapes

Flamouriana

1564m
Katharo
Tsivi

**Agios
Nikolaos**

Mohlos

Exo
Mouliana

Tourlot

Georgios

Lato

Ammoudara

Platanos

Sfaka

Skordilo

Avdeliakos

Kritsa

**Panagia
Kera**

Kolpos
Mirambellou

Kavousi

O r n o
1237m
Askordalia

Dafni

t

1485m
Platia
Korifi

Kroustas

Pahia
Ammos

Kalo Horio

Hrisopigi

akano

Males

Kalamafka

Stavros

Gournia

Monastiraki

Orino

Stavrohori

Ag Stefanos

etaxohori

o Simi

Makrilia

T h r i p t i s

Ag Ioannis

Makrygialos

Riza

Anatoli

Kendri

Kato Horio

Koutsouras

Silvolagos
esa

Mournies

Ammoudares

Gra Ligia

Vaïnia

Ferma

Mavros
Kolimbos

Mirtos

Nea Mirtos

Ierapetra

Nisi Chrisi

D

E

F

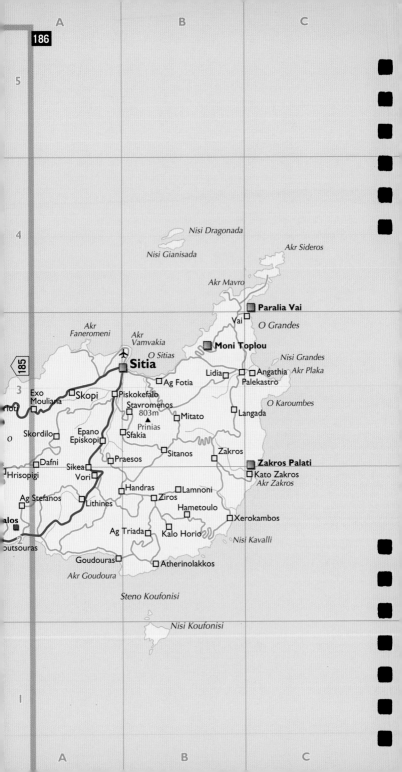

Nisi Dragonada

Nisi Gianisada

Akr Sideros

Akr Mavro

Akr
Faneromeni

Akr
Vamvakia

O Sitias

Paralia Vai

Vai

O Grandes

Moni Toplou

Nisi Grandes

Akr Plaka

Sitia

Ag Fotia

Lidia

Angathia

Palekastro

Exo
Mouliana

Skopi

Piskokefalo

Stavromenos

803m

Mitato

Langada

O Karoumbes

Skordilo

Epano
Episkopi

Prinias

Sfakia

Zakros

Zakros Palati

Dafni

Sikea

Vori

Praesos

Sitanos

Kato Zakros

Akr Zakros

Hrisopigi

Ag Stefanos

Lithines

Handras

Lamnoni

Ziros

Hametoulo

Xerokambos

alos

utsouras

Goudouras

Ag Triada

Kalo Horio

Atherinolakkos

Nisi Kavalli

Akr Goudoura

Steno Koufonisi

Nisi Koufonisi

SPIRALGUIDE
Questionnaire

Dear Traveller

Your comments, opinions and recommendations are very important to us. So please help us to improve our travel guides by taking a few minutes to complete this simple questionnaire.

You do not need a stamp (unless posted outside the UK). If you do not want to remove this page from your guide, then photocopy it or write your answers on a plain sheet of paper.

Send to: The Editor, Spiral Guides, AA World Travel Guides,
FREEPOST SCE 4598, Basingstoke RG21 4GY.

Your recommendations...

We always encourage readers' recommendations for restaurants, night-life or shopping – if your recommendation is used in the next edition of the guide, we will send you a FREE AA Spiral Guide of your choice. Please state below the establishment name, location and your reasons for recommending it.

_____

_____

_____

_____

_____

Please send me AA Spiral _____
(see list of titles inside the back cover)

About this guide...

Which title did you buy?

_____ **AA Spiral**

Where did you buy it? _____

When? m m / y y

Why did you choose an AA Spiral Guide? _____

_____

_____

_____

_____

Did this guide meet your expectations?

Exceeded ☐   Met all ☐   Met most ☐   Fell below ☐

Please give your reasons _____

_____

_____

_____

_____

continued on next page...

Were there any aspects of this guide that you particularly liked?

_____

_____

_____

_____

Is there anything we could have done better?

_____

_____

_____

_____

About you...

Name (Mr/Mrs/Ms) _____

Address _____

_____ **Postcode** _____

Daytime tel no _____ **email** _____

Please _only_ give us your email address and mobile phone number if you wish to hear from us about other products and services from the AA and partners by email or text or mms.

Which age group are you in?

Under 25 ☐ 25–34 ☐ 35–44 ☐ 45–54 ☐ 55–64 ☐ 65+ ☐

How many trips do you make a year?

Less than one ☐ One ☐ Two ☐ Three or more ☐

Are you an AA member? Yes ☐ **No** ☐

About your trip...

When did you book? mm/ y y   **When did you travel?** mm/ y y

How long did you stay? _____

Was it for business or leisure? _____

Did you buy any other travel guides for your trip? ☐ Yes ☐ No

If yes, which ones? _____

_____

Thank you for taking the time to complete this questionnaire. Please send it to us as soon as possible, and remember, you do not need a stamp (unless posted outside the UK).